# TABLE OF CONTENTS

D0074183

Copyright © Mometrix Media. You have been licensed one copy of this document for personal use only. Any other reproduction or redistribution is strictly prohibited. All rights reserved.

*Copyright © Mometrix Media. You have been licensed one copy of this document for personal use only. Any other reproduction or redistribution is strictly prohibited. All rights reserved.*

# Top 20 Test Taking Tips

1. Carefully follow all the test registration procedures
2. Know the test directions, duration, topics, question types, how many questions
3. Setup a flexible study schedule at least 3-4 weeks before test day
4. Study during the time of day you are most alert, relaxed, and stress free
5. Maximize your learning style; visual learner use visual study aids, auditory learner use auditory study aids
6. Focus on your weakest knowledge base
7. Find a study partner to review with and help clarify questions
8. Practice, practice, practice
9. Get a good night's sleep; don't try to cram the night before the test
10. Eat a well balanced meal
11. Know the exact physical location of the testing site; drive the route to the site prior to test day
12. Bring a set of ear plugs; the testing center could be noisy
13. Wear comfortable, loose fitting, layered clothing to the testing center; prepare for it to be either cold or hot during the test
14. Bring at least 2 current forms of ID to the testing center
15. Arrive to the test early; be prepared to wait and be patient
16. Eliminate the obviously wrong answer choices, then guess the first remaining choice
17. Pace yourself; don't rush, but keep working and move on if you get stuck
18. Maintain a positive attitude even if the test is going poorly
19. Keep your first answer unless you are positive it is wrong
20. Check your work, don't make a careless mistake

*Copyright © Mometrix Media. You have been licensed one copy of this document for personal use only. Any other reproduction or redistribution is strictly prohibited. All rights reserved.*

# Test Dates and Fees Breakdown

The CLA examination is offered three times a year: March/April (depending on the holiday schedule); July and December. Application forms and the requisite fees must be received by the published filing dates. Filing deadline dates are January 15 for the March/April examination, May 15 for the July examination and October 1 for the December examination session.

The fee for the CLA examination is $250 for NALA members and $275 for non-members of NALA.

National Association of Legal Assistants
1516 S. Boston
Suite 200
Tulsa, OK 74119
Fax: 918-582-6772
E-mail: nalanet@nala.org

*Copyright © Mometrix Media. You have been licensed one copy of this document for personal use only. Any other reproduction or redistribution is strictly prohibited. All rights reserved.*

# Test Breakdown

The CLA examination is divided into five sections. Examinees are asked to demonstrate knowledge by responding to true/false, multiple choice and matching questions requiring knowledge of the subject and reading comprehension skills. Analytical skills and writing abilities are further tested by essay questions. The sections of the examination are as follows:

## Communications

- Word usage and vocabulary
- Grammar/punctuation
- Writing skills
- Nonverbal communications
- General communications related to interviewing and client communications
- General communications related to interoffice office situations

## Ethics

- Ethical responsibilities centering on performance of delegated work including confidentiality, unauthorized practice of law, legal advice, conflict of interest, billing and client communications
- Client/public contact including identification as a non-lawyer, advertising and initial client contact
- Professional Integrity/competence including knowledge of legal assistant codes of ethics
- Relationships with co-workers and support staff
- Attorney codes/discipline

## Legal Research

- Sources of law including primary authority, secondary authority; understanding how law is recorded
- Research skills including citing the law; shepardizing, updating decisions; procedural rules of citations
- Analysis of research problem including identification of relevant facts and legal issues

*Copyright © Mometrix Media. You have been licensed one copy of this document for personal use only. Any other reproduction or redistribution is strictly prohibited. All rights reserved.*

**Judgment and Analytical Ability**

- Comprehension of data – identifying and understanding a problem
- Application of knowledge – ability to link facts or legal issues from other cases to the problem at hand, recognizing similarities and differences by analogy
- Evaluating and categorizing data
- Organizing data and findings in a written document

**Substantive law**

The substantive law section of the examination is composed of five sub-sections. The first section, Substantive Law-General covers concepts of the American legal system. All examinees are required to take this section. Subjects covered within this section include:
- Court system including their structure and jurisdiction
- Branches of government, agencies, and concepts such as separation of powers
- Legal concepts and principles including sources of law, judicial decision making, appellate process
- Sources and classifications of law including the constitution, statutes, common law, civil law, statutory law and equity law

The other four sub-sections are selected by the applications from a list of eight substantive areas of the law. These tests cover general knowledge of the following practice areas:
- Administrative Law
- Bankruptcy
- Business Organizations
- Civil Litigation
- Contracts
- Criminal Law and Procedure
- Estate Planning and Probate
- Real Estate

The skills required by these tests involve recall of facts and principles that form the basis of the specialty area. Examinees must also demonstrate an understanding of the structure of the law and procedures to be followed in each specialty area.

Copyright © Mometrix Media. You have been licensed one copy of this document for personal use only. Any other reproduction or redistribution is strictly prohibited. All rights reserved.

# Communications

## *Word Usage and Vocabulary*

**Commonly confused words**

<u>Then and than</u>
Novice writers often confuse *then* with *than*. These two words sound similar but have different meanings. *Then* is an **adverb** denoting a specific time. Here is an example of the correct usage of *then*: The robber removed his mask, and then we recognized him as Harry Mudd. *Than* is a **conjunction** used in comparisons. Here is an example of the correct usage of than: That Big Mac is more than I can finish at lunchtime. Ask yourself if your reader needs to know the sequence of what happened, and if so, use *then*. If your reader needs to know if something is bigger, smaller, or different, use *than*.

<u>Your and you're:</u>
Novice writers often confuse *your* with *you're*. *Your* and *you're* are **homonyms**— words that sound the same but mean something entirely different. *Your* is a **possessive pronoun** denoting ownership. Here is an example of the correct usage of *your*: Is that your new house?

*You're* is a **contraction** of the words *you* and *are*. Here is an example of the correct usage of you're: You're on the list of witnesses scheduled for Monday. When trying to decide whether to use *your* or *you're*, ask yourself if the sentence would still convey the correct meaning if you substituted *you are*.

> Correct: You are on the list of witnesses scheduled for Monday.
> Incorrect: Is that you are new house?

Remember, contractions are only appropriate for verbal conversations and casual correspondence. Do not use contractions in formal legal documents. Spell out the entire word for the sake of clarity.

<u>Their, there, and they're:</u>
*Their*, *there*, and *they're* are **homonyms**—words that sound the same but mean something entirely different.
- *Their* is a **plural possessive pronoun** denoting ownership by a group. Here is an example of the correct usage of *their*: It is their house because they own it.
- *There* is an **adverb** or **expletive**, as in:
  Damian is lying there asleep.
  There are three days left before his parole.
- *They're* is a **contraction** of *they* and *are*.

*Copyright © Mometrix Media. You have been licensed one copy of this document for personal use only. Any other reproduction or redistribution is strictly prohibited. All rights reserved.*

When trying to decide whether to use *their*, *they're*, or *there*, ask yourself if the sentence would still convey the correct meaning if you substituted *they are*.
**Correct:** They're going to the movies together. They are going to the movies together.
**Incorrect:** Their going to the movies. There going to the movies.

To, two and too:

Novice writers often confuse *to* with *two* or *too*, especially those with English as a second language. *Too, two* and *too* are **homonyms**—words that sound the same but mean something entirely different.

- *To* is a **preposition** that indicates movement in a particular direction, or a connection with a related verb, or a comparison, or a similar relationship between two words or phrases
- *Two* is a **number**
- *Too* is an **adverb** that means also or extremely

Here is an example of the correct usage of to, two and too:
Too many of your comments were directed to the audience, but the last two were directed to the jury.

Affect and effect:

*Affect* - usually a **verb** meaning to influence, touch emotions, infect with disease, or make a pretentious display. Accent the last syllable (a-FFECT):

> *Ex: "Inflation can affect the value of the U.S. dollar. "*
> *"Pleas from the arsonist's mother did not affect my testimony."*
> *"The rich Texan affected a French accent."*

*Affect* can also be a **noun** in psychiatric reports that describes the prisoner's body language and facial expression. Accent the first syllable (AFF-ect) when *affect* is a noun, for example: Norman's flat affect is caused by his schizophrenia.

*Effect* is a usually a **noun** meaning a result, for example: When the robber pointed his gun at the children, the effect was that their eyes filled with tears.

> *Effects* are personal possessions.
> *Ex: Sound effects* and *special effects*

*Effect* can be a **verb** meaning to cause or create, for example: Only the President could effect such an economic change.

Cite and site:

*Cite* and *site* are **homonyms**—words that sound the same but mean something completely different. *Cite* is a **verb** meaning to refer to or to quote. Legal citations are a standard language that refers the reader to the court decisions and other

*Copyright © Mometrix Media. You have been licensed one copy of this document for personal use only. Any other reproduction or redistribution is strictly prohibited. All rights reserved.*

sources used by the author. Legal citations use abbreviations to save space, for example: *Cmty. for Creative Nonviolence v. Reid*, 490 U.S. 730 (1989). Keep one of these reference manuals handy to ensure you cite correctly in your documents: *The Bluebook, ALWD Citation Manual* or *Universal Citation Guide*. *Site* is a **noun** meaning a specific location, such as a murder site or accident site. It is important to remember the difference between these two words, as they are both extremely common in legal writing. Choosing the wrong homonym changes the meaning of an entire sentence, or worse, an entire document.

<u>Who, whom, which, and that:</u>
Who can only be used as the **subject** of a sentence or a subject complement, as in: *Who* went to the office yesterday? *Whom* can only be used as the **object** of a sentence, as in: That's the man with *whom* I rode yesterday. Both *who* and *whom* refer to people. Never use *which* to refer to a person; *which* refers to a thing.
**Correct:** Fans cheered the injured player, *who* limped as he was assisted from the field.
**Incorrect:** Fans cheered the injured player *which* limped as he was assisted from the field. Fans cheered the injured player *that* limped as he was assisted from the field.
*That* can refer either to a thing or to a group of people, as in: The team *that* scores the most points in this game will represent the U.S.A. at the Olympics.

## Connotation vs. denotation

The connotation of a word is its emotional or figurative association *and* its literal meaning. The denotation of a word is only its literal or dictionary meaning. For example, a child can be called a minor, an infant, a fetus, a descendant, a juvenile delinquent, a kid, a baby, a son, a daughter, a stepchild, or a youngster. Although all of these words denote child, they have very different connotations. Your choice of words depends on the exact legal meaning you are trying to convey and your target audience. Avoid prejudicial terms. It is important for the paralegal to consider a word's connotation before using it because the implied (unstated) meaning can work against your client.

## Colloquialisms

Colloquialisms are casual words or phrases used in informal conversation. For example, a student says colloquially to his friend, "The test was nowhere near as hard as I thought." When the student speaks to his employer, he says formally, "The test was not as difficult as I expected." Casual words like *y'all, gonna* and *wanna* are colloquialisms appropriate for informal verbal conversations only. Colloquial usage varies from one part of the country to another, but legal terminology must be consistent throughout the U.S.A. Do not use colloquialisms in legal documents or formal conversations with employers, clients, law enforcement officers, and court officials.

*Copyright © Mometrix Media. You have been licensed one copy of this document for personal use only. Any other reproduction or redistribution is strictly prohibited. All rights reserved.*

## Slang terms

Slang terms are used by specific social groups, such as gang members, prisoners or soldiers, to mean something different from the term's established meaning. Slang is a transient trend or insider joke. For example, a "Blob" is a Crips' gang slang term for a Blood gang member.

Copyright © Mometrix Media. You have been licensed one copy of this document for personal use only. Any other reproduction or redistribution is strictly prohibited. All rights reserved.

# Grammar/Punctuation

## Comma use

In names, dates, addresses and numbers.
> *Example*: John Jackson, M.D., performed the surgery on July 2, 2007, at his Oakland, California clinic for $5,550.

After an introductory word group.
> *Example*: If Joe wants to win, he must practice every day.

Before a coordinating conjunction.
> *Example*: The dog barked loudly, but stopped when we gave him a bone.

To avoid confusion.
> *Example*: Incorrect: If you cook John will do the dishes. Correct: If you cook, John will do the dishes.

Between items in a series.
> *Example*: We ordered pancakes, bacon, eggs, and orange juice.

Between cumulative adjectives.
> *Example*: Helen is a bright, friendly, confident girl.

Before a nonrestrictive noun or pronoun.
> *Example*: Murray wants to vacation in Las Vegas, which is too expensive.

Around an adjective clause.
> *Example*: The defendant's apartment, which is on the tenth floor, overlooks the plaintiff's patio next door.

Around an appositive.
> *Example*: Michael Jackson's 1982 release, *Thriller*, sold 109 million copies.

After a transitional expression.
> *Example*: We lined up for the movie; however, there were no tickets left when we reached the cashier.

## Colon use

After the salutation in a formal letter, in time, proportions, titles, bibliographies, and Bible verses
> Dear Mr. Expert Witness:
> Please come to the courthouse at 8:30 a.m. Monday. The ratio of men to women on the jury will be 3:1. You will testify about your book, *Understanding Creole:*

*Copyright © Mometrix Media. You have been licensed one copy of this document for personal use only. Any other reproduction or redistribution is strictly prohibited. All rights reserved.*

*Different Strategies*, Toronto: Nelson Thomson Learning, 2009. You will explain how Luke 10:22 relates to the defendant's case.

<u>After an independent clause to draw attention 3 to a list</u>
Your daily exercise routine consists of the following: Running 5 miles, 100 sit-ups, lifting 200 pounds, and swimming 10 lengths.

<u>Before a quotation</u>
Consider the words of William Ramsay Clark: "Who will protect the public when the police violate the law?"

<u>Before appositives</u>
Our client is guilty of only two of the five misdemeanors: Trespass and vandalism.

<u>For a summation</u>
The appeals were ultimately useless: our client was incarcerated at Draper Correctional Facility.

## Semicolon use

<u>Between independent clauses</u>
Mencken said, "Injustice is relatively easy to bear; what stings is justice."

<u>Between independent clauses linked with a transitional expression</u>
We want to buy a house in New York; moreover, we specifically want to live in Brooklyn.

<u>Between items in a series with internal punctuation</u>
Major religious texts include the New Testament, authored by the Apostles; the Koran, authored by Mohammed; and the Talmud, authored by groups of rabbis.

<u>When a coordinating conjunction, such as but, is omitted between independent clauses</u>
Most American hospitals offer only Western medicine; Chinese hospitals offer both Eastern and Western medicine.

## Hyphenation

<u>Connect two or more adjectives before a noun</u>
Joe Smith is not a well-known lawyer. The car skidded across the snow-covered ground. The arsonist lit the oil-soaked rag.

<u>Join the numerator & de-nominator of a written fraction</u>
One-fourth, three-sevenths, two-fifths

*Copyright © Mometrix Media. You have been licensed one copy of this document for personal use only. Any other reproduction or redistribution is strictly prohibited. All rights reserved.*

Join two job titles
    writer-editor, carpenter-engineer

Write compound numbers from 21 to 99
    Twenty-one, thirty-six, ninety-nine

Joining titles of relatives
    great-uncle, great-grandmother

Compound words containing the prefixes all, ex, quasi, or self
    All-knowing, ex-wife, quasi-scientific, self-help

Compound words contain-ing the suffix elect
    John Doe is now president-elect.

Compound words, especially with awkward double letters
    Cross-examine, cross-stitch, 19-century, long-distance, newspaper-wrapped, co-ordinate, anti-intellectual

At the end of a line to divide words at syllables
    Re-
    cognize

## Italics

Italics are *slanted typeface* in printed documents.  Underlining is equivalent to italics in handwritten or typewritten documents.  Italics emphasize a word or phrase, so use them sparingly. Italics can also denote a proper name for the following publications:  Magazines, books, newspapers, pamphlets, poems, plays, films, TV or radio programs, musical compositions, choreography, painting titles, comic strips, and computer software. Use quotation marks for a short story, song, short poem, or essay.  Use italics or underlining for foreign words in an English sentence.  However, if the foreign word is accepted in common usage, do not italicize it.  Examples of common foreign words that are not italicized are habeas corpus and per diem. Use italics when introducing or defining a new word in a text, or to denote a word is being used as an example.  Italics denote a character's thoughts, whereas quotation marks denote speech.  Italics are used in symbols for mathematical variables. Italicize the names of spacecraft, ships, trains, and aircraft.

## Quotation marks

Rules for correct quotation mark use:
Enclose the speaker's exact words.  If one speaker utters more than one paragraph, place quotation marks at the beginning of the first paragraph and end of the last paragraph only.

Copyright © Mometrix Media. You have been licensed one copy of this document for personal use only. Any other reproduction or redistribution is strictly prohibited. All rights reserved.

*Example*: Justice Stone told reporters, "The Chapman ruling sets a precedent for future prostitution cases."

Less than 50 words: use quotation marks. Longer than 50 words or more than 2 paragraphs, indent 10 spaces from left margin.
*Example*: According to Subsection 5 of The Highway Traffic Act, "Parked vehicles shall not remain unattended in a loading zone more than five minutes."

Place colons and semicolons outside quotation marks.
*Example*: Mr. Murphy wrote, "I regret I am unable to attend the fundraiser"; however, he enclosed a $200 check in the envelope.

Place question marks and exclamation marks inside quotation marks unless they apply to the whole sentence.
*Example*: The actual lyric is, "When will I see you again?" Do you know the proverb, "Revenge is a dish best eaten cold"?

Titles of articles, poems, short stories, songs, TV episodes, radio programs, and book chapters.
*Example*: Robert Burns wrote "Auld Lang Syne".

Place periods and commas inside quotation marks.
*Example*: "Put your hands in the air," said the officer. "Turn around."

Use single quotes for a quote within a quote.
*Example*: The informant said, "McLaughlin told me, 'I killed her in the kitchen!'"

**Apostrophe use**

Write words out in legal documents. Contractions can be misinterpreted.
    can't/cannot, it's/it is, won't/ will not, 'twas/was

To indicate *singular* possession
*Rule:* If the noun does not end in *s*, then add *'s*.
    lawyer's desk; Joe's and Mary's *separate* lawsuits    *Exception:* Possessive pronouns its, his, hers, etc.,

To indicate *singular* possession: If the noun ends in *s*, use only if *'s* would make pronunciation difficult
    Lois'; Jacques'; students'; Stephanos'; James' (James's is used in the UK.)

To indicate *joint* possession
    John and Mary's *shared* home

*Copyright © Mometrix Media. You have been licensed one copy of this document for personal use only. Any other reproduction or redistribution is strictly prohibited. All rights reserved.*

Compound nouns
> Mary inherited her dead father-in-law's house.

Indefinite pronoun
> Anyone's license can be revoked for speeding. Somebody's briefcase was left in the courtroom.

Numbers, letters, and abbreviations
> '60s flower children; skating figure 8's; seats in the D's; check their I.D.'s
> *Exceptions:* Plurals such as 1980s, VCRs, IUDs

## Brackets [ ]

Relevant clarification
> Mr. Meadows indicated the amount by pointing to the price tag [$9.99].

Indicate you inserted your own words into a direct quote
> *Audubon* reports that "if DDT contamination continues to thin their egg shells, the [Peregrine falcon] species will become extinct".

Indicate an error made by the speaker in a quote with the Latin word *sic*
> Mr. Johnson wrote, "I seen [*sic*] Jimmy stab the guard before he fell."

## Parentheses ( )

Provide supplemental information as an afterthought.
> The paramedic measured the plaintiff's blood pressure, pulse, and temperature (part of a routine assessment) and she did not complain about him touching her at the time

Number a series of items
> Prison regulations allow only the following possessions in the cell: (1) a bed, (2) one blanket, (3) one towel, (4) one washcloth, (5) one tin cup, (6) one bucket, (7) and a Bible or another religious book approved by the Warden.

Indicate the page in a book citation or a date in a case citation
> Henry Abraham, *Justices and Presidents*, 350–356, 3rd ed. (1992).
> Murphy v. McMaster, 75 U.S.L.W. 4297 (U.S. Apr. 30, 2009).

## Dash —

Emphasizes parenthetical material
Before and after a list of appositives that contains commas
To amplify, restate, or shift thoughts

*Copyright © Mometrix Media. You have been licensed one copy of this document for personal use only. Any other reproduction or redistribution is strictly prohibited. All rights reserved.*

*Examples:*
Everything that occurred—from the overdose to the head-on crash—Helen blamed on my poor parenting.
Paella—Spanish dish containing rice, seafood, chicken, pork, vegetables and saffron—is prepared in a wide, shallow fry pan.
Consider the average American's height and weight gain—one inch taller and 25 pounds heavier now than in 1960, according to the CDC.

**Ellipsis ...**

Indicates you deleted words from a verbatim quotation. If you removed a full sentence or more from the center of a quoted passage, insert a period before the three ellipsis dots. Ellipsis also indicates an interrup-tion or unfinished thought.
    *Example:* Murphy reports that "when the blood alcohol concentration (BAC) rises above 0.35 grams per 100 milliliters...the patient can die".

**Ending punctuation**

Exclamation marks:
An exclamation mark indicates strong feeling. Place *one* exclamation mark at the end of a sentence only. Do not use multiple exclamation marks for emphasis. Use exclamation marks for a strong command, the description of a loud noise, or to indicate surprise, as in these examples:
- "Ready, set, go!"
- Bang!
- Oh no!

Exclamation marks are only necessary when something extreme occurs, so use them sparingly.

Period:
A period indicates the end of a sentence. Periods also indicate that certain titles and terms are abbreviated. For example, Junior is abbreviated to Jr. and Senior is abbreviated to Sr. Periods are required for some, but not all abbreviations, so check your legal stylebook.

Question marks:
A question mark indicates an answer or thought is required. Example: Do you think you'll pass the exam without studying?

*Copyright © Mometrix Media. You have been licensed one copy of this document for personal use only. Any other reproduction or redistribution is strictly prohibited. All rights reserved.*

## Grammar terms

| Definition | Example |
|---|---|
| A **proper noun** is a name for a person or place and is capitalized. | *Jane* is going to the party in *Gainsborough*. |
| A **common noun** is a thing, idea, person or place and is not capitalized. | The *mouse* ran into the *hole*. *Mouse* = subject; *hole* = object |
| **Adjectives** modify nouns. | You can't make a *silk* purse from a *sow's* ear. |
| **Articles** precede nouns to mark them as definite (*the*) or indefinite (*a* or *an*). | *The* tree on your right is a sycamore. *A* tree gives shade. |
| A **pronoun** substitutes for a specific noun, called the pronoun's antecedent. | When the *dog* barked, *it* was fed. *Dog* = antecedent; *it* = pronoun |
| **Personal pronouns** substitute for people or things | *I, me, you, we, they, he, she, her, him, they, us, them* and *it*. |
| **Verbs** express action or being. | Sharks *swim* constantly. |
| A main verb can have a **helper verb** that is a version of *have, do* or *to be*, or a **modal verb** like *can, could, ought, might, must, shall, should, will* or *would*. | Rome *was* not *built* in a day. *Was*, the helper verb for *built*, is the past tense of *to be*. |
| **Adverbs** modify verbs, adjectives, or other adverbs. Adverbs answer how, when, where, and why. | Tug *gently* at the sticker. Be *extremely* quiet, or we'll be *very* noticeable. *Never* tell a client your boss *always* wins his cases. |
| **Prepositions** precede nouns and pronouns to modify another word in the sentence. | The road *to* hell is paved with good intentions. We continued studying, *despite* our fatigue. |
| **Note:** Prepositions include *above, after, beneath, before, concerning, considering, despite, during, except, for, from, inside, into, like, near, next, of, off, opposite, past, plus, regarding, round, since, than, throughout, to, underneath, unlike, with,* and *without*. | |

Remember, a **specific noun** is better than a pronoun for legal documents. *Correct:* The defendant said he went to see the 9:10 *movie.*
*Incorrect:* The defendant said he went to see *it* at 9:10.

*Copyright © Mometrix Media. You have been licensed one copy of this document for personal use only. Any other reproduction or redistribution is strictly prohibited. All rights reserved.*

**Verbs**

<u>Helping verbs:</u>
A helping verb is a form of *be*, *do*, or *have*. It can also be a modal: *Can, could, may, might, must, ought to, shall, should, will,* or *would.* A helping verb appears before the main verb to establish mood or tense. For example, the modal *can* is a helping verb that establishes the tense of the main verb *go* in this sentence: She *can* go tomorrow.

<u>Mood:</u>
English has three moods:

- Imperative mood for orders or advice, as in: *Alert* your newspaper delivery boy that you will be away for a week.
- Indicative mood for opinions, questions, or facts, as in: The police officers advised against allowing workmen access to our house without proper I.D.
- Subjunctive mood for wishes, requests or contrary conditions, as in: If I *were* the judge, I would sentence him to life imprisonment.

<u>Tense:</u>
**Tense** refers to the time of the action.

- Past: I was.
- Present: I am.
- Future: I will be.

**Adverb and adjectives**

Determine whether a descriptive word is an adverb or an adjective simply by looking at its ending. Adverbs usually end in *ly* but adjectives usually do not. Examples of adverbs are *correctly, carefully, gracefully,* and *quickly*. Examples of adjectives are *correct, careful, graceful,* and *quick*. However, not every word ending in "ly" is an adverb and not every word without the "ly" ending is an adjective. For example, the word *well* is actually an adverb because it describes the way that an action is performed. Remember, adverbs answer how, when, where, why, to what degree, or under what conditions an action occurs. Adjectives answer how many, what kind, or which one.

**Articles in grammar**

The three articles in English are: The **indefinite articles** *a* and *an*, and the **definite article** *the*. Indefinite articles refer to *any* object, place or person, as in *a tree, a dock,* or *a boy*. The definite article refers only to *specifics*, as in *the flower, the runway,* or *the teacher*. Use *a* before a consonant sound, as in *a pear*. Use *an* before a vowel sound, as in *an* apple. The exceptions are words that begin with *h*. If the *h* is silent, as in *hour, heir,* and *honest,* then treat the word as if it begins with the second letter, which is a vowel. Therefore, *an hour, an heir,* and *an honest* are correct.

*Copyright © Mometrix Media. You have been licensed one copy of this document for personal use only. Any other reproduction or redistribution is strictly prohibited. All rights reserved.*

However, if the *h* is pronounced, as in *hotel, hymn,* and *hospital,* then treat the word as beginning with a consonant. Therefore, *a hotel, a hymn,* and *a hospital* are correct. Do not use *a* or *an* with a noncount noun. For example, do not write: James asked his lawyer for an advice.

## Conjunctions

<u>Coordinating Conjunctions:</u>
A coordinating conjunction links two or more words, clauses, or phrases of similar importance together. The coordinating conjunctions used in the English language are *and, but, for, nor, or, so,* and *yet.*
<u>Subordinate Conjunctions:</u>
A subordinate conjunction is a word or phrase that links the main clause of the sentence with another less important clause. Subordinate conjunctions include *after, although, because, if* and *unless.*

## Interjections

An interjection is a word that describes a strong feeling or a command. Interjections may appear separate from a sentence if they are followed by an exclamation point or as part of a sentence with a comma and/or an exclamation point. Some examples of interjections are "No!", "Hey!", and "Wait!"

## Capitalization

There are five instances when you must capitalize the first letter of a word:
1. The first word in a sentence.
2. A proper name of a person, language, group, major holiday, month, place, or thing, as in *Uncle Antoine, English, Shriners, Christmas, May, Washington,* and *Great Depression.*
3. The first or last word in a title or an important word in a title, as in *Book of Jeremiah.*
4. The singular pronoun *I* or one of its contractions, as in *I'd* or *I'll* or *I'm.*
5. The first word in a quotation if it starts with the beginning of a sentence, but not if it starts from the middle of a sentence. If the quotation begins with an ellipsis (...), do not capitalize the first letter.

## Dangling participles

A dangling participle is a sentence structure error in which a modifier is misplaced. The dangling participle does not refer logically to the word it is supposed to change, so that the meaning of the sentence is unclear. Consider this sentence: Leaving the office, Mike's leather jacket got soaked.

*Copyright © Mometrix Media. You have been licensed one copy of this document for personal use only. Any other reproduction or redistribution is strictly prohibited. All rights reserved.*

The participial phrase *leaving the office* is a dangling participle because it is not clear if Mike was leaving the office, if someone else was leaving the office with Mike's jacket, or if the jacket somehow left the office by itself. Other examples of dangling modifiers are:

- Though only 14, Georgia tried the boy as an adult.
- Upon seeing the police barricade, our car swerved into the driveway.
- To please the client, the paralegal's documents were delivered a week early.

**Misplaced modifier**

A misplaced modifier is a sentence structure error in which a word or phrase designed to change another word appears in the wrong sequence. A misplaced modifier makes it difficult for the reader to understand what the author intended. Place modifiers in front of the words they modify whenever possible and keep related words together. Consider this sentence containing a misplaced modifier:
*The judge returned to the courtroom where he handed down his famous Gideon v. Wainwright decision in 1991 in a limousine sent by the Office of the President.*
Here the reordered sentence structure makes the author's meaning clear:
*Riding in a limousine sent by the Office of the President, the judge returned to the courtroom where he handed down his famous Gideon v. Wainwright decision in 1991.*

Copyright © Mometrix Media. You have been licensed one copy of this document for personal use only. Any other reproduction or redistribution is strictly prohibited. All rights reserved.

**Legal writing**

Legal documents must be clear and unambiguous for the lawyers, clients, law enforcement officers, and judges who read them. The paralegal must know how to identify the parts of a sentence and use grammar correctly, so that contracts and other documents he/she writes comply with legal standards.

Concise:
It is important for legal writing to be as concise as possible for two primary reasons:
1. Clarity — The reader understands a short, concise writing more easily and quickly than long, wordy, poorly structured, ill-defined and confusing writing. Remember that the lawyers' arguments, judge's decision, and court's time may rest on your writing.
2. Formality — Concise writing almost always appears more formal, interesting, and intelligent than repetitive, wandering writing.

As a legal writer, try to be as concise and direct as possible. Note, however, that this does not mean that a legal writer should sacrifice content. Rather, a good legal writer should convey the necessary information in as few words as possible. Remember that most newspapers are written for a Grade 8 reading level, and even specialty magazines are not usually written above the Grade 12 level.

**Business letters**

The four formats commonly used in business letters are as follows:
- Full block style: Each line of text begins at the same starting point on the left margin. This style is the most modern and popular.
- Modified block style: A modified block style letter uses the same setup as the full block style letter with the exception of the date, the closing, and the line for the signature. Each of these three lines is located at the center of the page.
- Modified block style with indents: A modified block style letter with indents uses the same format as the modified block style, but the first line of each paragraph is indented and the subject line is either indented or located in the center of the page.
- Simplified style: A variation of the full block style in which each line of text begins at the same starting point, but the address line, the subject line, and the writer's name and title line are in capital letters.

*Copyright © Mometrix Media. You have been licensed one copy of this document for personal use only. Any other reproduction or redistribution is strictly prohibited. All rights reserved.*

<u>Punctuation styles:</u>
Here are the punctuation styles in use in the U.S.A. in order of frequency:

| 1. **Mixed** | No punctuation at the ends of inside address lines<br>Colon after the greeting or salutation<br>Comma after the complimentary closing |
|---|---|
| 2. **Open** | No punctuation at the ends of inside address lines<br>No punctuation after the greeting/salutation or the complimentary closing |
| 3. **Closed** | Commas at the end of each inside address line except the last one before the postal code<br>Period after the date and identification lines<br>Comma after complimentary closing and company name |

Ask your supervisor whether mixed or open style is preferred at your office, so that your work as a new employee is consistent with your colleagues'. Closed punctuation is used more for foreign correspondence outside the U.S.A.

## E-mail etiquette

The competent legal assistant ensures e-mails for professional purposes meet the same standards as business letters regarding appropriate grammar, punctuation, sentence structure, and correct spelling. However, e-mails are usually shorter than hard copy letters. If you have a lengthy document to discuss, make it an attachment, rather than including it in the body of an e-mail. Make it clear that you are not actually a lawyer, whether in the body of the e-mail or in the signature. Include a legal disclaimer at the end of the e-mail, stating it is for the intended recipient only and what to do if it is received in error. Avoid these two e-mail practices for legal work:

1. Do not use any abbreviations or symbols popular in casual e-mails, such as *IMO* for "in my opinion", or emoticons/smilies, (e.g., =) happy face symbol).
2. Avoid including confidential information in e-mails whenever possible, as it is difficult to ensure that the recipient will be the only person reading the e-mail.

# Nonverbal communication

## Nonverbal communication

Nonverbal communication is the way an individual creates a certain image and provides information to others without speaking, through posture, gestures, interpersonal space, facial expression, body language, eye contact, and clothing. *Appropriate nonverbal communication varies according to cultural expectations and the individual's state of health.* Nonverbal communication is mostly unconscious and spontaneous, and it makes up 85% of all communication.

*Copyright © Mometrix Media. You have been licensed one copy of this document for personal use only.*
*Any other reproduction or redistribution is strictly prohibited. All rights reserved.*

<u>Body language:</u>
Body language is the gestures, postures, expressions, and movements an individual uses to convey emotions, health, and mental state. An effective public speaker uses body language to keep the audience's attention. Professional and effective body language for the paralegal simply involves sitting up straight, keeping arms and legs uncrossed, avoiding excessive hand gestures, and maintaining a smile or empathetic expression, as appropriate.

<u>Eye contact:</u>
Eye contact is individual's ability to gaze at another person's eyes to show attention, gather information and as a social signal. The appropriate length of gaze varies according to culture, health, gender, age, distance, emotion, and if objects of mutual interest are present.

## Interviewing and Client Communications

### Legal interviews

The two types of legal interviews that a legal assistant or lawyer conducts are client interviews and witness interviews. Client interviews are any conversations in which a lawyer representing a customer, or a designated legal assistant, asks the customer for information about the case at hand. The lawyer or legal assistant asks the client to describe the facts of the case and displays empathy. The ethical duty of confidentiality and the rule of evidence concerning lawyer-client privilege apply to the initial interview, even if the client decides not to hire the lawyer, or if the lawyer decides not to accept this case. Witness interviews are conversations in which a lawyer or a legal assistant ask an individual whom the lawyer does not represent for information about the case. The interviewer reviews the file first before assessing the witness' credibility and presentation style and takes a statement.

<u>Conducting an interview:</u>
The two main ways that an interview can be conducted are in-person or over the phone. In-person interviews are face-to-face meetings in which a lawyer or legal assistant speaks with the client or witness is in the same room to gather necessary information for the case. In-person interviews are usually more effective than a telephone interview because the legal assistant or lawyer bonds with the client or witness and establishes trust by showing empathy. The interviewer must not interrogate the interviewee. The interviewer evaluates the client's or witness' facial expressions and body language to learn if he/she will be credible in court. Phone interviews show no non-verbal clues, so are less useful than in-person interviews. However, phone interviews are less time-consuming than interviews conducted in-person.

*Copyright © Mometrix Media. You have been licensed one copy of this document for personal use only. Any other reproduction or redistribution is strictly prohibited. All rights reserved.*

Showing concern for client:

Although the characteristics that an interviewer must emphasize vary from interview to interview, there are certain requirements that apply to all interviews. Demonstrate genuine concern while conducting an interview to establish trust and bond with the client. Explain lawyer-client privilege to the client. The lawyer's and legal assistant's first responsibility is always to their client, not to the family member who pays for the case. Remember, most clients only seek out a lawyer when they experience some sort of legal problem; rarely is he visit preventative. Although you may reassure the client, never promise the client that the lawyer will get them out of that situation, or state the lawyer always wins his/her cases.

Being courteous:

Courtesy is a characteristic required for all interviews. Remember that your client and his/her family are under stress because of the legal issue, social embarrassment, and associated costs. Therefore, they may not retain what you say, and you may need to repeat yourself. You and your principal need accurate, timely information from your client and witnesses in order to proceed with the case. Probe gently for information and be persuasive. Avoid interrogating or judging your client or witnesses and do not make false promises. Most individuals are reluctant to share information with an interviewer who is rude or inconsiderate, so be as courteous as the situation allows. Lawyers and legal assistants need clients to stay in business and rely on word-of-mouth recommendations. Alienating clients or potential clients through rude or inconsiderate behavior is never a good business tactic, and could result in your dismissal.

Positive attitude:

A positive attitude is a requirement for all professional interviewers. Your attitude is conveyed in your body language and tone of voice, more than the content of your speech. Encourage and reassure your client, but do not make false promises or exaggerated claims. Do not project doom and gloom or panic at the seriousness of your client's situation; speak in a well-modulated, calm voice. Never minimize your client's response as an overreaction. The interviewer who presents to the client and witness as positive and professional will receive more cooperation than the interviewer who is arrogant, judgmental, condescending, or patronizing. Treat each client or witness as a person of equal intelligence and importance to you. If you require a translator, sign language interpreter, or special needs worker to go forward with the interview, get one as quickly and pleasantly as possible and do not show irritation. Learn to recognize your interviewee's comfort and interest levels.

Environment:

The two environments in which an interview can be conducted are in the office and in the field. An **in-office interview** is held in the law firm's conference room or the individual lawyer's or paralegal's office. The benefit of an in-office interview is that the interviewer can control and manipulate the environment. It is easy to maintain privacy, confidentiality and sound levels. Equipment such as a photocopier, tape

Copyright © Mometrix Media. You have been licensed one copy of this document for personal use only. Any other reproduction or redistribution is strictly prohibited. All rights reserved.

recorder, camera and reference material are handy to make the first interview comprehensive. The client and witnesses may reveal more information because they are outside their comfort zones. A **field interview** is conducted in a location over which the interviewer has only limited control. There are many distractions to contend with in a hospital room, jail cell, accident scene or crime scene. The interviewer must work to be heard and yet maintain confidentiality. It is inappropriate to take photos and recordings in a coffee shop, for example. Lack of equipment may mean the interviewer needs to return for a second interview.

Preparing for an office interview:
There are three major things that should concern an interviewer who is preparing for an office interview:
1. Image: Are the office environment, staff, and interviewer's personal appearance clean, quiet and professional? Do not intimidate, discourage, disgust or overwhelm the interviewee. Maintain a separate waiting area away from the interview area.
2. Privacy: Can you protect your client from eavesdropping, wiretapping, intrusions and the press? Ensure that your client's information is stored in a confidential manner and is never disclosed to third parties. Remember that garbage is routinely searched by reporters, police, business competitors, and criminals.
3. Seating: Are there enough seats and can they be placed around the table at 45 angles? It is formal, old-fashioned and not conducive to open discussion when the interviewer sits behind a desk. A round table is best because it conveys cooperation. Sitting aslant from the client is non-confrontational, modern, and makes for better eye contact. An angled seating arrangement allows you to take notes easily.

*Office interview vs. field interviews:* An office interview is inconvenient for the client but preferable for the interviewer. At an office interview, the interviewer manipulates the space, lighting, seating arrangement, color scheme, privacy screens, noise level, distractions and temperature. Background music playing softly in the waiting room obscures the receptionist's conversation with the arriving visitor from eavesdroppers. A pink room temporarily calms agitation for about 20 minutes. (Hospitals and detention centers use color to influence mood.) A first interview requires a small, intimate setting, such as the lawyer's office. If the meeting is formal and includes the opponent's lawyer, then a large conference room is appropriate. The interviewer knows the emergency exits and safety alarms in his/her own space. Field interviews are more convenient for the client but put the interviewer at a disadvantage. Uncontrollable people, excess noise, and more distractions present than in a conference room or office.

- 27 -

*Copyright © Mometrix Media. You have been licensed one copy of this document for personal use only. Any other reproduction or redistribution is strictly prohibited. All rights reserved.*

Interview room:
Stock the interview room with the following items:

- Business cards: Provide clients and witnesses with you own and your principal's cards, so they can retrieve your contact information quickly.
- Rolodex: Keep referral information for reliable businesses handy, e.g., accountant, private detective, doctor, women's shelter, real estate broker, jewelry appraiser, and restoration service.
- Checklists: Keep yourself on task, on budget, and on schedule, and ensure you cover all essential information with the help of checklists. Microsoft offers many free checklists that you can tailor at http://office.microsoft.com/en-us/templates/.
- Forms: LawSmart.com offers many free standardized legal forms and guides for download, including bail bonds, workers compensation, tax, estates, and lemon law.
- Steno pads for taking notes of the key points in interviews (1 per case).
- Black pens for signing contracts.
- Photocopier for duplication within the client's sight, so you can return documents immediately.
- Clock for timekeeping and billing.
- Digital camera for recording evidence.
- Tape recorder for your transcriptionist.

Pitfalls:
These are the pitfalls to avoid in an interview:

- False Statements: Never state or imply that the lawyer or law firm will be able to achieve a certain outcome for the client. No outcome is guaranteed and it is inappropriate to lull your client into a false sense of security. Explain to the client what you are legally and ethically permitted to do.
- Overstepping Boundaries: The professional legal assistant or paralegal never offers his or her own opinion about anything related to the case. You are there as a facilitator and intermediary, not to practice law or issue judgments. Gather detailed information on the lawyer's behalf, convey his or her messages to the client, and report back an accurate account.
- Jargon: Explain any legal terminology you use in simple terms.
- Confusion & Delay: Avoid indirect or ambiguous questions whenever possible. Speak directly to the client first, rather than the caregiver. Do not use euphemisms or slang that could be misinterpreted.

Copyright © Mometrix Media. You have been licensed one copy of this document for personal use only. Any other reproduction or redistribution is strictly prohibited. All rights reserved.

## Conducting effective interviews

Here are the steps to an effective interview:
1. Determine what is already known about the case and identify the specific legal issues involved (e.g., DUI and grand theft),
2. Design a checklist of questions to gather information concerning the major legal issues of the case (e.g., Who, what, where, when, why and how),
3. Gather all necessary equipment and inform the receptionist of your whereabouts in case of misadventure,
4. Meet the client or witness in a suitable location and introduce yourself The distinct roles of lawyer and legal assistant, confidentiality rights, and the interview process,
5. Ask questions, using your checklist as a guide, and take notes (record if the client agrees),
6. Complete and sign forms and photocopy any required documents,
7. Allow the client or witness to ask questions before closing the interview with a recap and further instructions,
8. Document your interview for the lawyer,
9. Give the tape (if any) to the transcriptionist,

Questions:
The four types of questions that an interviewer may ask are:
1. Open questions ask the listener to explain something at length or describe something in general terms, for example, "Why were you in the jewelry store last Tuesday?"
2. Closed questions ask the listener to answer yes or no, or to give a short specific description, for example: "What color was the traffic light when you entered the intersection?" "Green." Closed questions do not elicit much information. Only use them when the witness tends to ramble or when speed is essential.
3. Leading questions are dangerous, because the interviewer suggests the answer that he or she wants the client or witness to provide, for example, "You were in the store around 10:00 p.m., is that correct?" A judge will not allow leading questions in court.
4. Silent questions occur when the interviewer pauses after the interviewee stops talking, hoping the interviewee will become uncomfortable in the silence and volunteer more information without prompting.

Improving effectiveness:
Two of the most useful techniques an interviewer can use to improve the effectiveness of an interview are:
1. Adapting the interview to the interviewee, in which an interviewer changes the questions that he or she planned to use, so that each question is more appropriate for the specific type of interviewee. Recognize that each interviewee is different, so change your vocabulary, pace, and social distance

*Copyright © Mometrix Media. You have been licensed one copy of this document for personal use only. Any other reproduction or redistribution is strictly prohibited. All rights reserved.*

accordingly.  If you need a translator, sign language interpreter, or special needs worker, book one ahead of time.   Make the interviewee as comfortable as possible.
2.  Allowing the interviewee to speak uninterrupted, in which an interviewer asks the question and does not speak again until the client or witness has finished talking.  This technique is extremely effective because it encourages the interviewee to provide as much information as possible in his or her own words.

Corroborating facts:
The two main types of facts that an interviewer must try to corroborate are details related to documents and details related to people.  **Details related to documents** include:  Prior verbal agreements to sign or change the document; the locations of buildings at the scene of the event; the work schedules of people at the event; and weather reports issued during the event.  **Details related to people** includes:  Identifying every individual involved in the event by name, address, hair color, eye color, clothing, facial features, body type, and height; why each individual was involved in the event; how each individual is related the others; and how often each individual was at the scene.

Active listening:
Active listening means the interviewer:
- Paraphrases the speaker and repeats back what he/she understood to confirm it.
- Asks for clarification when necessary.
- Watches for subtle visual clues indicating that a speaker is in pain, confused, lying, mistaken, or hiding information that may be useful.
- Uses visual clues as a catalyst for further questions.

Visual clues include grimaces, gestures, posture, hygiene and appearance.  The active listener considers if the interviewee's behavior is age-appropriate or precocious, and if it is right for the situation.  When the interviewee's speech and visual clues do not match, the active listener makes a mental note to investigate further.  The active listener asks open-ended questions and avoids leading the client or witness.  The active listener asks an expert when it is difficult to discern if an interviewee with a psychological problem has a nervous tic, or is genuinely distressed.

**Confabulation**

Confabulation means the interviewee creates details to fill in the missing pieces of a description or story.  The interviewee either does not know all of the facts involved in a particular situation, or does not want to describe the actual facts, so he/she invents plausible fine points to sound convincing.  The interviewee with a psychological disorder may believe his/her own confabulation.

Copyright © Mometrix Media. You have been licensed one copy of this document for personal use only. Any other reproduction or redistribution is strictly prohibited. All rights reserved.

## Contradictory statement

A contradictory statement is the opposite of what someone else said or the opposite of what the same individual previously said.

## External verification

External verification is confirmation performed by an independent third party through examination of documents. For example, an auditor's external verification of a firm's books is more credible in court than an internal verification.

## Internal verification

Internal verification is a quality assurance measure in which the firm evaluates its assessment practices to ensure they are appropriate, consistent, fair and standardized.

## Witnesses

The five types of witnesses that a legal assistant or a lawyer is required to interview are:
1. Expert witnesses — An individual with specialized knowledge of a technical field related to the case, such as a doctor, a forensics expert, a mechanic, or any other specialist.
2. Friendly witnesses — An individual who agrees with the client's point of view or who is a friend of the client.
3. Hostile witnesses — An individual who refuses to provide information the legal assistant or lawyer requests.
4. Neutral witnesses — An individual who has no relationship with the client or any other party involved in the case.
5. Official witnesses — An individual who holds a public office or works for a government department in a position of authority, such as a City Clerk, a Councilor, a park ranger, a police officer, or a deputy.

## Witness statement

A witness statement is a document or a recording detailing the witness' rendition of events. Witness statements document the information a witness provides that is later relied on in court. Begin with the name and address of the witness, the date and location in which the statement was made, the name of the interviewer and others present, the means used to identify the witness (e.g., a driver's license or nurse's verbal identification), and any information that authenticates the statement. Then present the witness' description of the event in his/her own words, a clause indicating the statement was provided willingly, and a signature clause indicating

Copyright © Mometrix Media. You have been licensed one copy of this document for personal use only. Any other reproduction or redistribution is strictly prohibited. All rights reserved.

the witness has no reason to believe that the information in the statement is inaccurate.

## Confidential conversations

It is appropriate for a legal assistant to tell a lawyer about a confidential conversation that the legal assistant had with a client, providing the lawyer represents that client, and the lawyer supervises that legal assistant. In fact, legal assistants are expected to inform their supervising attorneys of any information related to their clients, even if the client told that information to the legal assistant with the stipulation that it remain confidential. This is because lawyers can only act in the best interests of their clients if they have all of the necessary information. As a result, legal assistants are required to disclose confidential information to their supervisors. However, it is important to note that it is not appropriate for a legal assistant to disclose confidential information to anyone other than his or her supervising attorney, unless he or she is legally required to do so.

## Special interviewing situations

Interviewing the disabled:
Title VII of the Civil Rights Act of 1964, the Rehabilitation Act of 1973 and the Americans with Disabilities Act of 1990 affect how government services, landlords, businesses and employers interact with people with a physical or mental impairment that substantially limits a major life activity. You must provide the disabled interviewee with reasonable accommodations for special needs. If your office is not wheelchair accessible, interview at the client's home. Book a sign language interpreter, use a TTY or computer to conduct the interview if necessary. Allocate extra time for the accommodations.

Interviewing foreign language speakers:
If the interviewee is a non-native speaker, be sensitive to cultural differences. For example, Arabs find a social distance of one or two feet apart acceptable for conversations, but Asians prefer to talk at least three feet apart. East Indians may find it offensive to shake the left hand. In traditional Mexican families, the eldest male speaks for the interviewee. If language and idiom are barriers, then get a translation by phone or in person.

Interviewing children:
Interview a child younger than 5 years old in the presence of his/her parents. Keep the interview short for any child. Explain to every child the sequence and structure of the interview. Interview the child over 5 alone first, and then in the company of his/her parents. If their relationship is adversarial, you may want to interview the parents separately. Address adolescents as if they are adults; do not patronize an adolescent. Ask your minor client if there is any information that he/she prefers not be shared with his/her parents. It is

- 32 -

*Copyright © Mometrix Media. You have been licensed one copy of this document for personal use only. Any other reproduction or redistribution is strictly prohibited. All rights reserved.*

ethical to withhold this information from the parents, and it establishes rapport with the client.

<u>Interviewing the elderly:</u>
When interviewing an elder, ensure the location is accessible and that the elder has any necessary devices, such as a hearing aid, dentures, or glasses. Keep the interview short if the elder is ill or disabled. Ask the elder if he/she wants an attendant in the interview room, or to remain close by outside.

## Key terms

**Defenestrate:** Literally, to throw something or somebody out a window. Defenestrate can refer to attempted murder, or a political overthrow, or policy change, or exiting a computer window to improve system response, or using an ejection seat in an aircraft. Take the author's intended meaning from context.

**Defame:** To damage someone's reputation by slander (oral statements) or libel (written statements). Defaming a person exposes him or her to public ridicule or tarnishes his or her memory. The defamed person can lose business as a result of loss of his or her good name. A defamatory libel statement may be true, but is published maliciously (without just cause).

**Deforest:** To destroy trees, used when referring to logging operations, disease or insect attacks, climate change, or fires, as in: Global warming deforested millions of acres.

**Deprecate:** To belittle, depreciate, disparage, deplore, show disapproval, or discount the value of something, as in: The witness deprecated his testimony as unimportant to the verdict.

### Latin terms

**Ad curiam:** *To court*, interpreted as *before the district court*, as in: The judge ordered a publication ban while the matter is *ad curiam* so the jurors will not be influenced by news reports.

**Alibi:** *Elsewhere* or *in another place*. The suspect or defendant tries to prove he could not have committed the crime because he was elsewhere when it happened. Do not use *alibi* as slang for a ready excuse to avoid blame or justify actions.

**Circa:** *Round*, interpreted as *about the time* or *approximately the area*, as in: The original painting was made circa 1900 but the fake dates to 1970. It can also mean *concerning*.

**Flagrante delicto:** *Flagrant transgression*, used when perpetrators are caught red-handed while committing a crime, as in: The adulterers were caught in *flagrante delicto* by the detective and photographer.

**Ex parte:** *Out of party or faction*, interpreted as on behalf of only one party in a dispute, or without notice to the other party, or without a hearing.

**Adversus:** *Against*, abbreviated ADV. It refers to two parties that are opposing each other in a dispute.

Copyright © Mometrix Media. You have been licensed one copy of this document for personal use only. Any other reproduction or redistribution is strictly prohibited. All rights reserved.

**Contra:** *Contrary to.* Appears in *contra pacem* (against the peace), and *per contra* (to the contrary), and *contra bonos mores* (against good morals), and *contra formam statuti* (against the form of the statute).

**Inter alia:** *Among other things*, abbreviated IA. Note that this is not the same as *inter alios*, which means among other persons. *Inter* alia refers to something that occurred in addition to something else.

**Non obstante:** *Notwithstanding*, interpreted as in spite of, all the same, nevertheless, or although.

**Nota bene:** *Note well*, abbreviated as NB. Use NB to draw attention to information of significant importance.

**De facto:** *About fact*, interpreted as an actuality, as a matter of fact, or as a matter of law.

**Ex post facto**: *From within after the fact*, interpreted as after the act is done or after the fact.

**Ex delicto:** *Out of transgression,* meaning something occurred as the result of a wrongful act, which is a tort.

**Ipso facto:** *Fact by itself*, which refer to something that is proven or disproven by the fact that a particular act or event occurred.

**In loco parentis:** *In place of the parent*, meaning either the court appointed a guardian to act on behalf of the absent or negligent parents, or a healthcare provider is acting in the best interests of the child. For example, the triage team at an inpatient hospital can invoke an involuntary mental hold to evaluate a child for 72 hours for his or her own safety. The healthcare providers must not do this for financial gain or to comply with parental wishes.

**Ad damnum:** *To pen the loss*; in a civil action, the clause in the petition where the plaintiff outlines the damages he or she suffered and claims the amount of money he or she seeks as reparation.

**Ad hoc:** *To this*, meaning for a special reason only and not for general use. For example, an *ad hoc* committee is convened to consider one unusual case or for one emergency purpose, and will disband when the case or emergency is over.

**Bona fide:** *Good faith*, meaning an object is genuine or real, or a person acts sincerely, or business is conducted in an honest manner.

**Cestui:** *Person who benefits*, as in the beneficiary of a will or insurance claim.

**Corpus:** *Body.* A collection of laws or writings; principal as opposed to interest or income; a human or animal body; or the main body of a group, substance, or organ.

**Corpus delicti**: *Body of the crime,* a legal principle meaning the defendant cannot be convicted on the basis of his or her confession alone. The prosecutor must produce objective evidence that there was actually a crime committed.

**Habeas corpus**: *You have the body*, a writ ordering the custodian to bring the prisoner before the court or release the prisoner. It means the prisoner cannot be detained indefinitely and is entitled to a timely trial. Used as a method in federal court to try to overturn a criminal conviction when appeals have been denied at the state level.

**Prima facie:** *At first sight*, meaning apparently or superficially. *Prima facie* evidence is obvious and indisputable. No proof that the evidence exists is required.

*Copyright © Mometrix Media. You have been licensed one copy of this document for personal use only. Any other reproduction or redistribution is strictly prohibited. All rights reserved.*

## Legal terms

**Abatement**: A legal action that eliminates something or lowers an amount, for example:
- A judge quashes (abates) a charge because correct procedure was violated.
- A housing tribunal lowers (abates) a tenant's rent because his landlord failed to keep his apartment in acceptable condition.
- A beneficiary receives $5,000 less than specified in her uncle's Will because he sold a property at a loss before his death, so her bequest was abated.

**Acquittal:** When the accused in a criminal case is found not guilty, or when a respondent in a civil case is relieved of any debt or obligation.

**Sui generis**: *Born of itself,* meaning one-of-a-kind or without equal.

**Condemnation:** When the judge convicts the accused and passes sentence or inflicts a penalty. Can also mean expropriation, where the government seizes private property for public use.

**Conversion has three specific legal meanings:**
- In common law, when an individual seizes a rightful owner's property and stores it where the owner cannot recover it, or appropriates it for his own unlawful use.
- An Executor settles a Will by converting property from real to personal or vice versa.
- Financial officers convert foreign currency to U.S. dollars or precious metal, or convert securities from one class to another.

**Replevin:** A court order to return the plaintiff's wrongfully appropriated (converted) property. Also, a legal action where the plaintiff seeks to recover his actual property rather than its face value.

**Writ of Execution:** Also called an elegit. A court order instructing the sheriff to confiscate (levy) the debtor's bank accounts and property and award them to the creditor until the creditor's claim is satisfied.

**Estoppel:** a person cannot deny in court something already proven to be true. For example, the seller of a plot of land must accept the agreed-upon price stated in his real estate contract, even if he strikes oil the next day and the land is now more valuable.

**General Denial:** a legal pleading form the defendant completes in answer to the complainant's Statement of Claim, and mails to the Justice of the Peace or leaves with the Clerk of the Court. The defendant does not answer specific charges, just makes a blanket rejection of all claims and asks for a trial of the issues according to the appropriate civil rule. The defendant gives his or her contact information on the form.

**Motion in limine**: A lawyer makes a motion in limine to the judge, asking that a particular piece of information be ruled inadmissible to the jury, because it will create an unfair bias or is irrelevant.

*Copyright © Mometrix Media. You have been licensed one copy of this document for personal use only. Any other reproduction or redistribution is strictly prohibited. All rights reserved.*

# Sample questions

**Explain why the structure of the following sentence might be considered incorrect: The documents were filed yesterday by one of the office's legal assistants.**

This sentence is technically correct but considered poor form because it is written in the passive voice instead of the active voice. This simply means that the direct object, *documents*, and the verb, *filed*, come before the subject, *one of the office's legal assistants*. In almost every situation, the appropriate order in which to write the sentence would be subject, verb, and then direct object. The active voice would be easier to understand and livelier, as in: One of the office's legal assistants filed the documents yesterday. Passive voice is often used in medical reports and when trying to shift blame or obscure guilt. This is a typical sentence in passive voice: The blood pressure was taken by the nurse as necessary. This is a well-written sentence in active voice: The nurse took the patient's blood pressure every 15 minutes, starting at 10:00 a.m. until noon.

**Explain why the following sentence is incorrect: The clerk file the papers every day. Rewrite the sentence correctly.**

The clerk file the papers every day. This sentence is incorrect because the subject and verb do not agree in number. The subject, *clerk*, is a singular noun. The verb, *file*, is actually a plural verb, although it may appear to be a singular verb because there is no *s* ending. Remember that nouns are usually pluralized by adding an *s* at the end, but verbs are usually pluralized by subtracting the *s* at the end. Hence, if there is *only one clerk*, the sentence should read: The clerk files the papers every day. However, if there is *more than one clerk*, the corrected sentence reads: The clerks file the papers every day.

**Explain why the following sentence is incorrect: *When the clerk files the papers, they should always double-check the information.* Correct the sentence.**

*When the clerk files the papers, they should always double-check the information.* This sentence is incorrect because the subject, *clerk*, and the pronoun used to replace that subject, *they*, do not agree in number. *Clerk* is a singular noun. *They* is a plural pronoun. English speakers often misuse *they* in casual conversation to represent a single individual whose gender is unknown. However, *they* can only be correctly used to describe a group of people. *They* is incorrect in this particular sentence because the subject is one clerk. Replace *they* with *he or she* or *the clerk*. Either of the following corrections is acceptable:
1. *When the clerk files the papers, he or she should always double-check the information.*
2. *When the clerk files the papers, the clerk should always double-check the information.*

- 36 -

*Copyright © Mometrix Media. You have been licensed one copy of this document for personal use only. Any other reproduction or redistribution is strictly prohibited. All rights reserved.*

# Ethics

## *Ethical Responsibilities*

### Resources

A resource is anything that a legal assistant uses to achieve a particular objective. Human resources are also known as labor resources, and include anything related to the actual amount of time and effort that the legal team devotes to a particular task or objective. Billing is usually done hourly for human resources. For example, the billing department invoices the client for the total number of hours secretaries spend typing documents related to a case. Information resources include anything that allows a legal assistant to find and/or apply the knowledge necessary to complete a particular task or objective. Billing for information resources is usually on a flat fee basis. For example, the billing department charges a flat fee of 10 cents per copy for duplicating documents pertinent to the case. The legal assistant often devotes a couple of hours to a task and delegates simple, time-consuming tasks to a junior member of staff. The legal assistant checks back to ensure delegated tasks are completed on time.

Additional resources:
A legal assistant can determine if additional resources are required to complete a project by following these steps:
1. Identify the objectives.
2. Prioritize the tasks needed to achieve the objectives.
3. Estimate how much time it will take to complete each task.
4. List resources necessary to complete those tasks.
5. Identify the deadline by which time each task must be finished.
6. Determine if it is possible to complete the task independently or not.
7. Identify the resources that are available and determine if they are sufficient to complete the project
8. Get authorization for additional resources, if necessary.

The legal assistant tracks resource use for billing and supervises delegates to ensure budget and deadlines are met, and that the work is completed correctly.

Ensuring sufficient resources:
The situation may arise that you are unable to complete a task in the amount of time that is available. Use these two techniques to ensure that there are sufficient resources available to complete a project in the time allowed:
1. If it is impossible to complete the task because of competing tasks unrelated to the top priority case, then delegate the unrelated tasks to junior members of the office staff. Focus on the one crucial task that really needs to be

*Copyright © Mometrix Media. You have been licensed one copy of this document for personal use only. Any other reproduction or redistribution is strictly prohibited. All rights reserved.*

completed, instead of many minor tasks. Check regularly to ensure your
delegate is making progress and following correct procedure.
2. If it is impossible to complete the task in the time allowed because it is
simply too much for one person to handle, ask senior staff for help. The
lawyer may be able to get an extension.

## Professional ethics

Professional ethics refers to a collection of standard behaviors that a certain group
of professionals are expected to follow. Professional ethics are general principles,
values, and responsibilities that an individual must follow in order for his or her
behavior to be considered appropriate for a given field.

An ethical code is a collection of written rules that establishes which behaviors are
acceptable or unacceptable for a given profession. The code identifies very specific
behaviors so each member of the profession may preserve a certain level of
integrity. The National Association of Legal Assistants (NALA) and the American
Bar Association (ABA) establish most of the ethical codes that apply to legal
assistants and lawyers within the United States.

## Ethical responsibilities of a legal assistant

The two primary ethical responsibilities of a legal assistant are to remain competent
and to avoid any action that could be considered an unauthorized practice of law.
Legal assistants are expected to have the knowledge, skills, and abilities necessary
to carry out the legal tasks that they perform. Legal assistants are expected to
remain current, and to preserve and improve their knowledge through continuing
education. Continuing education can be meetings, seminars, and workshops, in
addition to formal lectures and examinations. The National Federation of Paralegals
Association requires 12 hours of continuing education every two years. The
National Association for Legal Professionals requires 75 hours of continuing
education for recertification. Legal assistants are prohibited from performing illegal
actions. Therefore, a legal assistant must be familiar with the laws pertaining to his
or her area of practice *and* any related federal laws governing the practice of law as
a whole.

Understanding lawyer's ethical rules:
A paralegal must understand the ethical rules governing a lawyer because they
apply to both workers. The paralegal's misconduct or negligence is considered the
lawyer's fault. Both workers must uphold the integrity of the legal profession. The
lawyer is the Principal who must supervise the paralegal and other staff to ensure
their performance is ethical. The paralegal has a duty to obey the Principal, to keep
safe property entrusted to the Principal, and to observe rules and laws governing
presentation. The paralegal must be courteous and operate in good faith with the

*Copyright © Mometrix Media. You have been licensed one copy of this document for personal use only.*
*Any other reproduction or redistribution is strictly prohibited. All rights reserved.*

Principal. Paralegals cannot offer independent counsel or misrepresent themselves as lawyers to clients. Business cards must show the name of both the paralegal and the Principal.

## Unauthorized practice of law

Legal assistants are allowed to perform a number of different tasks related to the field of law, but there are some specific tasks that they simply cannot perform. These forbidden tasks, known as unauthorized practices of law, vary from state to state. However, some specific tasks that legal assistants will almost never be able to perform are:
1. Accepting a client's case.
2. Providing legal advice directly to a client.
3. Negotiating a settlement or another similar legal issue for a client.
4. Representing a client in court for any legal matter.
5. Setting fees for the legal services provided to a client.

Most states have established regulations prohibiting legal assistants from taking the actions mentioned above and there are a number of penalties that legal assistants may face for taking these actions.

Penalties:
Legal assistants who take part in an action considered an unauthorized practice of law may face a number of different penalties including, but not limited to:
- Termination of employment by the employer.
- Civil penalties (fines and damages for negligence).
- Criminal penalties (custodial sentence).

The lawyer for whom the legal assistant works may also be held responsible for his or her legal assistant's unlawful practice of law, and may face civil penalties, such as damages for negligence or disbarment.
Even if a legal assistant is convicted of an unauthorized practice of law and is fired, he or she may still apply for another legal assistant position.

## Performing legal tasks

Legal assistants are allowed to perform a vast number of different tasks related to the field of law, but there are three requirements that must be met in order for them to perform these tasks:
1. A legal assistant must be working under the supervision of a licensed attorney before he or she may perform any legal task
2. The attorney who is supervising the legal assistant's work must establish a relationship with the client and preserve that relationship with direct contact throughout the legal assistant's dealings with the client. Hence, it is the

Copyright © Mometrix Media. You have been licensed one copy of this document for personal use only. Any other reproduction or redistribution is strictly prohibited. All rights reserved.

attorney's responsibility, *not the responsibility of the legal assistant*, to discuss the case with the client.

3. The attorney who is supervising the legal assistant must assume full responsibility for the legal assistant's work.

## *Client/Public Contact*

### Identification as non-lawyer

The legal assistant must make it clear that he or she is not a lawyer when dealing with:

- Potential clients.
- Existing clients.
- Individuals he/she deals with on a professional basis, such as police, court officials, detectives, law office staff, reporters, social workers, and healthcare providers.
- Opponents in a case.

The legal assistant is specifically prohibited from allowing other individuals to believe he/she can practice law independently, without oversight from the Principal. For example, if the lawyer is late for a court appearance, an experienced legal assistant cannot function in the lawyer's stead, even for a few minutes. It does not matter that the assistant has all of the required papers, researched the details of the case, is familiar with the client, and is well versed in courtroom procedure. Both lawyer and assistant would be subject to disciplinary action.

### Advertising

Newspapers:
It is ethical for a lawyer to advertise his or her services in a newspaper. In fact, a lawyer may advertise through any written or recorded communication. Advertising options include newspapers, radio, posters, flyers, Internet and TV. Remember that the advertisement must meet these three conditions to be considered ethical:

1. The ad must identify at least one of the lawyers responsible for the information included in the advertisement.
2. The ad must comply with all of the ethical rules pertaining to the information it contains.
3. The lawyers responsible for the ad must keep a copy for two years from the date that the advertisement was last shown or mailed.

Contacting potential clients:
A lawyer is prohibited from directly contacting an individual for the purpose of obtaining employment, unless the individual is an existing client or a relative. For example, if a lawyer represents a client in a house purchase, it is acceptable to

Copyright © Mometrix Media. You have been licensed one copy of this document for personal use only.
Any other reproduction or redistribution is strictly prohibited. All rights reserved.

follow up with a letter asking if the client has thought about changing his/her Will to reflect the new asset. A lawyer can solicit a relative for work. However, it is unethical for a lawyer or a representative of the lawyer's office to cold-call potential clients. The lawyer may use a recorded message with an autodialer, provided:

1. The recipient did not previously object to the message.
2. It is the first time that the potential client received the message.
3. The message makes it clear at its beginning and end that it is an advertisement.

Mail:

Lawyers cannot contact an individual directly for the purpose of obtaining employment, unless that individual is an existing client or relative. However, it is ethical for a lawyer to send advertisements to potential clients, providing *Advertising Material* is clearly printed on the outside of the envelope. The potential client must receive only one copy of that particular advertisement. The lawyer cannot bombard the recipient with multiple copies of the same ad. It is unethical for a lawyer to mail an advertisement if the envelope is not clearly marked *Advertising Material* or if the lawyer believes the potential client has already received a copy earlier.

Paying referral fees:

In most cases, it is unethical for a lawyer looking for work to pay referral fees. Lawyers are specifically prohibited from offering referral fees to any private individual or private for-profit organization. However, a lawyer may pay another organization to create classified or display advertising for the lawyer's practice, providing those fees are only related to the advertising itself and not to any referral service. It is also important to note that a lawyer may pay a non-profit organization for any referral services it offers. For example, a lawyer who specializes in domestic violence cases may enter into a referral contract with a non-profit women's shelter. The lawyer must pay no more than the normal fee charged by the organization.

**Admitting lack of knowledge**

It is ethical for the lawyer to admit lack of knowledge in a particular area of law. The lawyer need not tell the applicant outright that he or she lacks the required knowledge, or does not accept cases in a particular area of law, unless concealing that information violates a law or an ethical responsibility. Refer the applicant to your local law society, or to another lawyer who is knowledgeable in that area. Most law societies operate a **lawyer referral service** to connect clients with three appropriate lawyers. The service is not affiliated with Legal Aid and cannot arrange fees. Usually, if the prospective client tells the referral lawyer the contact information was provided by the service, then the first 30 minute consultation is free. The client and lawyer are not obliged to work together.

*Copyright © Mometrix Media. You have been licensed one copy of this document for personal use only. Any other reproduction or redistribution is strictly prohibited. All rights reserved.*

## Claiming specialization

It is unethical for a lawyer to state that he or she is a specialist in a specific area of law *unless* the lawyer is a patent attorney or an attorney handling admiralty law.

## Name of a law firm

In most situations, it is unethical for a lawyer to use his or her name as part of the name of a law firm if the lawyer holds a public office. Law firms are prohibited from including the name of a public officer in the firm's name if he/she does not practice with the firm on a regular basis. The work connection cannot be intermittent or casual. However, it is acceptable for a firm to use the name of a lawyer in a public office as part of the name of the firm if the lawyer is still an *active member* of the firm, who works there on a regular basis.

## Partnerships

It is unethical for a lawyer to state that he or she is in a partnership with another lawyer *unless* an official partnership exists between the two lawyers. A lawyer cannot say that he or she is a partner simply because both lawyers are related, or work in the same building, or share office space as co-tenants, or both accept referrals from a non-profit agency.

## Creating a firm name

It is unethical for a lawyer to create a firm name or letterhead that makes the firm's lawyers sound more experienced than they actually are. This is because lawyers are specifically prohibited from creating any professional designation, such as a name or letterhead, which provides other individuals with information that the lawyer knows to be false or misleading.

# *Attorney Codes/Discipline*

## Competent representation

Competent representation is one of the primary ethical responsibilities of a lawyer. It means the lawyer must only represent clients in cases that the lawyer knows how to handle. The lawyer must be at least somewhat familiar with the applicable laws, statutes, regulations, and precedents pertaining to the case. If the lawyer lacks the necessary background, then he or she is obliged to choose one of these three options:
1. Refuse the case.
2. Affiliate with a lawyer who is familiar with the appropriate area of law.
3. Study the area of law related to the case, providing there is sufficient time to do so.

*Copyright © Mometrix Media. You have been licensed one copy of this document for personal use only. Any other reproduction or redistribution is strictly prohibited. All rights reserved.*

## Client's rights

A lawyer is ethically required to allow his or her client to make independent decisions regarding representation. This means that a lawyer must allow his or her client to decide if he or she wants to:
- Accept a settlement
- Enter a plea
- Testify in court
- Waive his or her right to a trial by jury
- Take an action that might negatively impact another individual

It is important to note, however, that *a lawyer is specifically prohibited from taking any action that would constitute fraud or a criminal act.* If a client asks a lawyer to take part in an illegal action, then the lawyer must refuse to take part and inform the client that all lawyers have this same ethical responsibility.

Right to confidentiality:
Lawyers are ethically responsible for protecting their clients' privacy in almost every situation. A lawyer is specifically prohibited from providing another individual with any information related to a client's case, or any other legal matter for which the lawyer is representing the client, *unless the client agrees to the disclosure.* Lawyers are prohibited from discussing the client or the client's case with any other lawyers who do not need to know the information. A lawyer cannot provide other individuals involved in the dispute with more information than is necessary. The lawyer cannot tell others that the client is being represented by his law firm, unless the lawyer is certain that it is a matter of public record. Note that a lawyer can disclose information without a client's consent providing it is necessary in order to represent his or her client. The client's right to privacy is the responsibility of both the lawyer *and* the legal assistants who work for that lawyer.

*Exceptions:* Lawyers are required to protect their clients' privacy in *almost* every situation. The following are situations in which a lawyer is required to provide information to another individual, even though the client has not consented, and/or disclosing the information is not required to represent the client:
1. Warning an individual or group regarding a client's intentions to prevent an attack or criminal act that could result in serious injury or death.
2. Informing authorities that the client committed perjury without the attorney's prior knowledge.
3. Providing information to an individual or group to aid in the defense of the lawyer when a client takes civil action against the lawyer for alleged misrepresentation.
4. Providing information to an individual or group to aid in the defense of the lawyer if criminal charges have been filed against the lawyer.

*Copyright © Mometrix Media. You have been licensed one copy of this document for personal use only. Any other reproduction or redistribution is strictly prohibited. All rights reserved.*

**Ethical responsibilities of a lawyer**

A Client's Right to Diligence:
A client's right to diligence refers to the ethical responsibility of the lawyer to carry out the tasks related to a particular case in a timely fashion. The lawyer is required to meet all of the necessary filing deadlines related to a particular case. The lawyer must take steps to ensure the case proceeds as quickly as realistically possible. Legal assistants play a pivotal role in helping the lawyer meet due diligence requirements.

A Client's Right to Be Informed:
A client's right to be informed refers to the ethical responsibility of a lawyer to ensure a client has all of the information that he or she needs. Lawyers must inform their clients when events occur that may affect the case. Lawyers must provide information to clients who request it, and explain the information fully to the client. Legal assistants help the lawyer fulfill this duty through researching information for clients and creating status letters.

**Lawyer's fee**

Lawyers must adhere to three ethical rules related to their fees:
1. Lawyers are prohibited from charging unreasonable fees, which means that a lawyer cannot charge a fee that is disproportionate to the amount of work performed, or to the lawyer's experience. As a result, a lawyer's fee must be based on the time that the lawyer spent handling the case, the deadlines related to the case, the difficulty of the case, the lawyer's level of experience, the lawyer's reputation, and whether the lawyer achieved the desired outcome or not.
2. Lawyers must inform their clients of the fees that will be charged at the earliest time possible. If there are any contingent fees, the lawyer must inform his or her client of those fees in writing.
3. If multiple firms handled the same case, the fees related to the case can only be divided if the client agrees. The division must be based on the amount of work performed by each firm, or the firms must agree how they will share responsibility for the client's representation.

Accepting a portion of a client's business:
In certain circumstances, it is ethical for a lawyer to accept a portion of a client's business as payment for services rendered. The lawyer cannot take part in any transaction in which the lawyer gains partial or total ownership of a client's business, unless:
1. The client had the opportunity to seek legal council from an individual other than the lawyer.
2. The terms of the agreement are reasonable.
3. The client agrees to the terms of the agreement.

Copyright © Mometrix Media. You have been licensed one copy of this document for personal use only. Any other reproduction or redistribution is strictly prohibited. All rights reserved.

It is also important to note that it is unethical for a lawyer to enter into any arrangement in which he or she would receive something other than a contingency fee or a lien to cover fees and expenses, if the lawyer's receipt of that payment is based on the outcome of the case.

Accepting a gift:
In most cases, it is unethical for a lawyer to accept a gift for services rendered or to accept any agreement in which the lawyer would receive a gift for services rendered. In fact, lawyers are prohibited from taking part in any transaction in which the lawyer or a relative of the lawyer receives a gift from a client, unless the client is a relative of the lawyer. It is also unethical for a lawyer to accept payment from anyone other than his or her client, in most cases. This is because a lawyer is prohibited from accepting payment from anyone other than his or her client unless the client's right to confidentiality is upheld, the lawyer does not enter into any arrangement with the individual paying the lawyer's fee, and the client agrees.

Contingency fee:
A contingency fee, or a contingent fee, is payment a lawyer receives *if* he or she wins the client's case. The client is not required to pay if the lawyer loses the case. A lawyer may require a client to pay a contingency fee as long as the lawyer adheres to three ethical rules:
1. The lawyer must inform the client of the contingency fee and its associated terms *in writing* at the earliest possible time.
2. The fee must follow all of the other ethical rules associated with lawyers' fees, including but not limited to, reasonable rates.
3. The case for which the contingency fee is charged must be a *civil case* unrelated to alimony, child support, property distribution resulting from a divorce, or obtaining a divorce.

**Conflicts of interest**

It is the ethical responsibility of a lawyer to act in the best interests of his or her client for any case that the lawyer agrees to accept. It is usually impossible for a lawyer to act in the best interests of two opposing parties. Therefore, lawyers are prohibited from representing two or more opposing parties in the same legal matter. This rule also applies to legal assistants who work for multiple lawyers. If you work as legal assistant for a firm where two different lawyers represent the two opposing parties involved in the same case, then you cannot assist both lawyers with the case. With this information in mind, it is important to note that a lawyer may represent two opposing parties *if both parties agree that it is acceptable for the lawyer to represent the opposing parties and there is no reason to believe that either party will be negatively impacted by the lawyer's decision to represent both parties.*

*Copyright © Mometrix Media. You have been licensed one copy of this document for personal use only. Any other reproduction or redistribution is strictly prohibited. All rights reserved.*

## Accepting settlements or pleas

It is unethical for a lawyer to accept a settlement for more than one client involved in the same civil case, or to accept a plea agreement for more than one client involved in the same criminal case, unless two separate conditions are met:
1. Each client involved in the civil or criminal case must be made aware of the fact that the lawyer is representing more than one client, and each client must agree that it is acceptable for the lawyer to represent more than one client in that particular case.
2. Each client involved in the settlement or the plea agreement must be informed of the terms of the settlement or agreement and how those terms will affect each of the clients that the lawyer is representing for that particular settlement or agreement.

## Offering financial aid for a pending civil case

In most cases, it is unethical for a lawyer to offer financial aid to a client involved in a pending civil case. This is because lawyers are specifically prohibited from offering financial aid to a client awaiting a pending claim, unless that financial aid is in the form of an advance for court costs and expenses.

## Writing a book about a client

Lawyers are required to protect their client's right to confidentiality whenever possible. As such, it is unethical for a lawyer to obtain or attempt to obtain the book rights or the rights to any other creation depicting his or her representation of a client.

## Limiting liability

Lawyers are ethically responsible for the actions they take on a client's behalf. As a result, it is unethical for a lawyer to ask a client to limit any liability that the lawyer may face due to the lawyer's actions.

## Representing a mentally impaired client

The lawyer must act in the best interests of his or her client, and furnish the client with accurate, understandable information to make decisions. The lawyer must ask the court to appoint a legal guardian for a mentally disabled or temporarily impaired client, if it is clear that close oversight is in the best interests of the client. This is true only if the client *obviously* cannot make appropriate independent decisions. For example, a depressive who is well-controlled on medication, or a trainable intellectually disabled person with mild Down syndrome who lives independently, are probably both capable of self-determination. The lawyer

*Copyright © Mometrix Media. You have been licensed one copy of this document for personal use only. Any other reproduction or redistribution is strictly prohibited. All rights reserved.*

monitors the guardian's actions throughout any legal matter in which the lawyer represents that client, to ensure they remain in the client's best interests.

## Holding another's private property

A lawyer may hold another individual's property, providing three specific rules are followed regarding storage:
1. The property must be stored in a separate location from the lawyer's property.
2. Held money must be deposited into a separate bank account from the lawyer's account, in the same state as the lawyer's office, and the lawyer must keep a record of the deposit.
3. If a lawyer receives money or property for another individual, the lawyer informs the new owner, keeps a record of all property received, and presents the money or property to the new owner as soon as possible.

## Refusing a client

The three situations in which a lawyer is ethically required to refuse a client or to immediately discontinue representing a client are as follows:
1. The lawyer is unable to represent the client due to a physical or mental condition that impairs the lawyer's ability to perform his responsibilities.
2. The lawyer would violate a law or ethical code by representing the client.
3. The client terminates his relationship with the lawyer.

If a lawyer is required to refuse a client or to discontinue his or her representation of a client for any of these reasons, then the lawyer must inform the client as soon as possible.

## Filing frivolous lawsuits

The lawyer has an ethical responsibility to avoid any lawsuit or issue that could be considered frivolous. The lawyer is specifically prohibited from filing nuisance lawsuits. The lawyer cannot place facts into a lawsuit that have no realistic use, other than to injure or annoy another individual.

## Observing rights of third persons

The lawyer must act in the best interests of the client whenever possible. However, the lawyer has an ethical responsibility to observe the rights of third parties, even if the client might benefit from the violation of those rights. The lawyer is prohibited from taking any action that would violate the legal rights of another individual, or any action that has no realistic use other than to annoy, delay, embarrass, or injure another individual.

*Copyright © Mometrix Media. You have been licensed one copy of this document for personal use only. Any other reproduction or redistribution is strictly prohibited. All rights reserved.*

## Making false statements to officials

It is the lawyer's ethical responsibility to provide accurate information to officials whenever possible. The lawyer is prohibited from:
- Making any statement to an official that the lawyer knows to be false.
- Concealing any information that may lead to criminal or fraud charges against the lawyer and/or the client.
- Offering evidence the lawyer knows to be false.
- Concealing any legal authority, even if that authority may negatively impact the lawyer's client.

## Influencing officials

The lawyer has an ethical responsibility to act in a fair and professional manner. The lawyer is prohibited from:
- Bribing an official of the court.
- Taking any action that might influence an official of the court.
- Speaking with an official of the court outside of the court proceedings, unless the lawyer's right to do so is established by law.

## Delaying a case

The lawyer can deliberately delay a case if doing so would be in the best interests of the lawyer's client. For example, if the lawyer believes that he or she may be able to find additional evidence to aid his or her client's case, but the lawyer needs additional time to find that evidence, it would be considered ethical for a lawyer to try to delay the case by whatever legal means necessary. However, if the lawyer has no reason to believe that a delay would be in the best interests of the client, it would be considered unethical for the lawyer to delay the case. The lawyer may delay a case if it helps his or her client, but a lawyer may not delay a case in order to aggravate another party, to artificially increase the fee that the lawyer will receive for his or her labor, or to achieve any other purpose other than helping the lawyer's client.

## Disclosure of evidence

The following are the ethical rules lawyers are expected to follow regarding the disclosure of evidence. The lawyer *cannot*:
- Conceal any evidence from another party, unless concealing that evidence is allowed by law.
- Change or damage any evidence.
- Take any action to prevent another party from accessing any evidence that the other party is legally entitled to access or use.

*Copyright © Mometrix Media. You have been licensed one copy of this document for personal use only. Any other reproduction or redistribution is strictly prohibited. All rights reserved.*

- File a discovery request or presenting information in court that is irrelevant or has no purpose other than to delay or aggravate another party.
- Offer any compensation to a witness for his or her testimony.
- Advise a third party to withhold information unless the third party is an agent, employee, or relative of the client and the lawyer has no reason to believe that the third party would be injured by his or her decision to conceal the information.

The lawyer must make a reasonable attempt to respond to any and all legitimate discovery requests in a timely fashion.

## Statements to the press

In certain circumstances, it is ethical for a lawyer to make a statement to the press outside of the courtroom. The circumstances in which it is *unethical* for a lawyer to make any press statement outside of the court room are to:
- Influence a pending civil case that may be tried by a jury.
- Influence a pending criminal case in which the defendant may face jail time if convicted.
- Comment on the character or the criminal record of a witness or the opposing party.
- Comment on the credibility of a witness.
- Comment on the reputation of a witness or the opposing party.
- Express opinions about the guilt or innocence or pleas of a particular party.
- Express opinions about test results or a party's refusal to submit to testing.
- State anything related to testimony that the lawyer believes will be presented by the opposing party.

## Testifying in a case

In most cases, it is unacceptable for the lawyer to represent a client in a case in which the lawyer may be asked to testify. In fact, the lawyer is specifically prohibited from accepting any case in which he or she is *likely* to be a witness. However, it is acceptable for the lawyer to represent a client in a case in which he or she may be asked to testify if one or more of these conditions apply:
- The lawyer is asked to testify about the services that the lawyer provided in another case.
- The lawyer is asked to testify about a piece of information that cannot be disputed.
- The lawyer's refusal to accept the case would cause the client significant hardship.

*Copyright © Mometrix Media. You have been licensed one copy of this document for personal use only. Any other reproduction or redistribution is strictly prohibited. All rights reserved.*

## Criminal prosecutor filing charges

The criminal prosecutor must ensure that the justice system operates in a fair and impartial manner. It is unethical for the criminal prosecutor to file charges without probable cause. In fact, a criminal prosecutor is specifically prohibited from filing charges without probable cause or taking any action that would unfairly influence a judge or jury. This means that a criminal prosecutor must gather sufficient evidence in support of the accused guilt *before* he or she files a criminal charge. Also, the criminal prosecutor must refrain from encouraging the judge or jury to decide on the basis of something other than the evidence against the accused.

## Discussing a pending case

The lawyer cannot discuss a pending case with the client's opposing party, if the opposing party is represented by another attorney. This no-contact rule applies to any and all forms of communication. The lawyer cannot take any action that would facilitate discussion of the case with an opposing party. However, the lawyer may speak with an opposing party providing their conversation is not related to the case in which the opposing party is involved or anything else that would violate a law or ethical code. It is also important to note that a lawyer may discuss a pending case with the opposing party involved in that case *if* the opposing party's attorney agrees.

## Discussing legal issues with unrepresented persons

Lawyers must make it clear that they are legal advisors *for hire*. The lawyer cannot offer legal advice or take action on behalf of any individual who is not a client because **rarely does the lawyer have a duty of care to non-clients.** The lawyer could be charged with **intentional misconduct** and might face disciplinary proceedings.

## Making false statements to third persons

The lawyer must provide accurate information whenever ethically required to do so, and whenever the lawyer receives a legal request for release of information. The lawyer is prohibited from making any statement to a third party that the lawyer knows to be false. The lawyer must not conceal any information in which the concealment of that information may lead to criminal charges or charges of fraud against the lawyer or the lawyer's client.

## Supervising the conduct of legal assistants

The lawyer must perform his/her own duties in a fair and ethical manner. The lawyer must also ensure that anyone he/she employs performs fairly and ethically, too. The lawyer is ethically responsible for overseeing the firm's legal assistants and

*Copyright © Mometrix Media. You have been licensed one copy of this document for personal use only. Any other reproduction or redistribution is strictly prohibited. All rights reserved.*

other auxiliary personnel to ensure they comply with all applicable laws and ethical codes.

## Practicing while unauthorized

It is the ethical responsibility of the lawyer to ensure his/her law practice is legally authorized. The lawyer cannot practice law in any jurisdiction in which he/she is unlicensed.

## Aiding in the unauthorized practice of law

The lawyer cannot aid an unauthorized individual to practice law. The lawyer is specifically prohibited from helping an unlicensed individual to practice law. This prohibition includes disbarred lawyers, graduates who have not yet been called to the bar, and those lawyers whose licenses have expired.

## Opposing a related lawyer

The lawyer must act in the best interests of his or her client. This means the lawyer avoids any case in which there is or might be a conflict of interests. The lawyer cannot accept a case in which the opponent is represented by a relative of the lawyer. However, the lawyer may represent a client in a case in which the opponent is represented by a relative of the lawyer *if* the clients know the lawyers are related and agree consanguinity is acceptable. The situation may make working conditions very difficult, particularly if the two attorneys work in the same office or are married.

## Champerty

An unethical agreement between a lawyer and a client or outside party. Champerty is buying into someone else's lawsuit. Champerty takes two forms:
1. The lawyer agrees to sue and pay the client's costs in exchange for a portion of the damages awarded. Supporting the client this way is called **maintenance**. Champerty became popular in the 1990s for personal injury lawsuits (ambulance chasing).
2. In common law, an uninterested outside party instigates the litigation for profit. A finance company promises the lawyer a share in the proceeds if the lawsuit succeeds. If the lawsuit fails, the finance company is liable for the costs.

Champerty was a crime and a tort, but is now legal in many jurisdictions. Champerty is illegal when the lawsuit involves public policy.

Copyright © Mometrix Media. You have been licensed one copy of this document for personal use only. Any other reproduction or redistribution is strictly prohibited. All rights reserved.

### Chinese wall

A Chinese Wall is a screening procedure designed to prevent conflict of interest. If a lawyer acts for Mr. Smith in financial matters, the same lawyer cannot act for Mrs. Smith in their subsequent divorce case because the lawyer is tainted.

### Offering reduced fees or free services

Free services are called *pro bono*, Latin meaning 'for good'. Lawyers are expected to offer reduced fees and *pro bono* services to charities, worthy individuals, or non-profit groups with extremely limited resources who cannot afford the lawyer's standard fees. *Pro bono* work is an accepted way for a new lawyer to establish a good reputation. There is no written code for the specific number of reduced fee or *pro bono* cases a lawyer must accept. However, each lawyer is ethically required to spend at least some time on pro bono work. If the lawyer is unable to work *pro bono* or chooses not to provide discount services personally, then the lawyer can fulfill this obligation by funding organizations that do offer them. Examples are National Veterans Legal Services Program, Minnesota Advocates for Human Rights Refugee & Asylum Project, and community organizations dealing with domestic violence, housing, employment, health, and bankruptcy.

### Limiting ability of another lawyer

It is the ethical responsibility of a lawyer to act in a fair and professional manner for all dealings. Fairness and professionalism extends not only to clients, but also to opponents, third parties, other lawyers and legal staff. A lawyer cannot enter into any agreement that limits the ability of another lawyer to practice law for any reason. The only exception is if a lawyer enters into an agreement with another lawyer regarding retirement benefits. A lawyer may create an agreement revoking retirement benefits if the signor leaves the law firm.

### Issuing competitive statements

A lawyer cannot make competitive comments that clearly state or imply he/she is more suited for a particular type of case than another lawyer, if that is untrue. The lawyer cannot claim to be capable of performing a task that he/she is not legally or ethically able to perform. The lawyer cannot suggest or claim he/she has a special skill for representing a certain type of client in a particular case that is superior to another lawyer's, unless that claim can be proven. It is unethical for a lawyer to state or imply he/she has a significant chance of achieving a particular outcome when that is not true.

*Copyright © Mometrix Media. You have been licensed one copy of this document for personal use only. Any other reproduction or redistribution is strictly prohibited. All rights reserved.*

# Ethical Standards

## ABA Model Rules of Professional Conduct

The American Bar Association's (ABA) Model Rules of Professional Conduct is a document describing all of the specific ethical rules that a lawyer is expected to follow.

## NALA Code of Ethics and Professional Responsibility

The National Association of Legal Assistants' (NALA) Code of Ethics and Professional Responsibility is a document describing all of the specific ethical rules that a legal assistant is expected to follow. These guidelines primarily establish that it is the responsibility of a legal assistant to avoid the unlawful practice of law, remain competent, and avoid any actions that would violate the ethical responsibilities of the lawyer whom the legal assistant serves (the Principal).

## NALA Model Standards and Guidelines for Utilization of Legal Assistants

The National Association of Legal Assistants' (NALA) Model Standards and Guidelines for Utilization of Legal Assistants is a document identifying the activities that a legal assistant can and cannot ethically perform.

Copyright © Mometrix Media. You have been licensed one copy of this document for personal use only. Any other reproduction or redistribution is strictly prohibited. All rights reserved.

# Legal Research

## *Sources of Law*

### Legal research

Legal research is a process whereby the legal assistant attempts to find information related to the legal rules that apply to a particular legal matter. The legal assistant uses a number of different resources to research the laws, regulations, and precedents applicable to a case. Legal assistants are often required to conduct legal research in order to find information that the lawyer may use to aid his or her client in a case. Legal research can be extremely time-consuming and legal assistants will usually only have a very limited amount of time to find all of the information required. Find all of the information relevant to a particular legal matter as quickly as possible, and ensure you use only reputable and up-to-date resources.

Preparation:
There are three main things that a legal assistant must determine before he or she begins the legal research process:
1. Determine to which court system the legal matter belongs—local, state or federal court. This is important because each court system is different and the laws, procedures, and precedents affecting the case may be different in each system.
2. Classify the legal matter as administrative law, case law, civil law, criminal law, or constitutional law.
3. Determine the rules related to the legal matter, such as court rules, evidence rules, procedural rules, and statutes.

Adequate preparation will save you research time.

### Legal rules

The two main types of legal rules, also referred to as legal authorities, are primary law and secondary law. **Primary law** is any legal rule recorded in an official government document, such as a case record, a court ruling, an executive order, the procedural rules associated with a particular legal matter, a state constitution, statutes, or the U.S. constitution. Legal rules that fall under the category of primary law are considered *binding* and they will usually be more useful in court than legal rules that are considered to be secondary law. **Secondary law** is any legal rule or any interpretation of a legal rule that is recorded in anything other than a government document, such as a legal dictionary, a legal encyclopedia, or a law textbook. Legal rules that fall under the category of secondary law are *non-binding* and the courts will always give more consideration to primary law than secondary

Copyright © Mometrix Media. You have been licensed one copy of this document for personal use only. Any other reproduction or redistribution is strictly prohibited. All rights reserved.

law. However, it is important to note that secondary law may still be useful in many cases.

**Primary law**

The two main types of primary law are Substantive Law and procedural law. **Substantive Law** refers to any law establishing the rights or responsibilities of the people to whom the law applies. For example, the right to free speech is a type of Substantive Law established in the U.S. Constitution. Substantive Law is found in executive orders, statutes, state constitutions, and the U.S. Constitution. **Procedural law** refers to any law establishing specific procedures that the judicial system and individuals interacting with the system must follow for each Substantive Law to be carried out fairly and consistently. Procedural law is often recorded in a number of different documents. The specific procedures required for a particular case can vary greatly from jurisdiction to jurisdiction.

Substantive law:
1. Common law — Substantive law established by a previous court decision, where a legal rule sets a precedent. Common law includes case law and is usually based on English law from the time of the American Revolution. The principle underlying common law is *stare decisis.*
2. Constitutional law — Substantive law established by a state constitution or the U.S. Constitution. State examples are found in the *Revised Statutes* or *Compiled Statutes.* Federal examples are found in the *Federal Register* and *Code of Federal Regulations,* such as regulations governing trade tariffs, taxes, the military, copyright, and patents. Constitutional law takes precedence over statutory law.
3. Executive order — Substantive law that is a directive of the President of the United States or a state Governor. Orders involve emergency powers necessary for wars, budget cuts, and water cuts during drought.
4. Statutory law — Any substantive or session law passed by a local, state, or federal legislative body. Federal statues take precedence over state statutes. State statutes take precedence over common law.

Procedural law:
The two main types of procedural law are federal procedural law and state procedural law. **Federal procedural law** is the legal rules the federal government established to ensure federal court continues to act in a fair and consistent manner. Federal procedural law is recorded in documents such as the *Federal Rules of Appellate Procedure,* the *Federal Rules of Civil Procedure,* the *Federal Rules of Criminal Procedure,* and the *Federal Rules of Evidence.* **State procedural law** is the legal rules that each state government established to ensure each state court continues to act in a fair and consistent manner. State procedural law is typically recorded in state statutes or court rules.

*Copyright © Mometrix Media. You have been licensed one copy of this document for personal use only. Any other reproduction or redistribution is strictly prohibited. All rights reserved.*

*Role of local court:* Most procedural law is established by the federal procedural rules set by the federal government or the state procedural rules set by the state government. However, local court rules often play an important role in procedural law because they establish more specific rules than the higher courts. For example, a paralegal might encounter a state procedural rule stating an appeal must be filed within 30 days from the date that the decision was rendered, but the rule does not list exactly which forms the paralegal must file for the appeal to go forward. The paralegal must check for the local jurisdiction's rules describing the specific forms necessary to file an appeal.

## Legal authorities

The United States Constitution:
The **United States Constitution** is a legal document that was primarily designed to establish the framework for the federal legal system. However, the U.S. Constitution has also often been used as a set of guidelines to establish the framework for the constitutions used by each of the 50 states. This means that the U.S. Constitution is essential to both the federal legal system and the state legal systems. As a result, the U.S. Constitution is rarely changed, but it has been amended occasionally. The articles and amendments of the U.S. Constitution can be found in the index of the United States Code.

State Constitutions:
Each state in the United States has its own **state constitution** with its own distinct set of laws. The laws established by each state's constitution and the manner in which each constitution is recorded varies greatly from state to state. However, most states include the constitution with the state's statutory code, so each state constitution is usually relatively easy to find.

Administrative agencies:
An administrative agency is a government organization designed to address a particular type of social or legal issue. An administrative agency often has the authority to establish rules and regulations regarding its jurisdiction or catchment area. There are many rules and regulations established by a wide range of administrative agencies, like Medicare, the Army Corps of Engineers, and the Securities and Exchange Commission. The rules and regulations of administrative agencies are published in the *Code of Federal Regulations* (C.F.R.), the *Federal Register* (Fed. Reg.), and in documents published by the agency itself.

Case law:
Case law usually refers to the practice of using precedent for *stare decisis*. A court record or a series of court records are quoted to prove a particular case. These records may include court decisions, court opinions, law reports, and similar documents that may indicate that a particular precedent has been set.

*Copyright © Mometrix Media. You have been licensed one copy of this document for personal use only. Any other reproduction or redistribution is strictly prohibited. All rights reserved.*

American Jurisprudence:
*American Jurisprudence* is a legal encyclopedia published by Lawyer's Co-op. *American Jurisprudence* is easier to read than other legal encyclopedias because the information included in it is written with as few footnotes and other interruptions as possible.

American law reports:
*American Law Reports* is a collection of annotated state case reports published by Lawyer's Co-op. *American Law Reports* does not include case reports for every state case, but concentrates on cases that may have a considerable legal impact. Each case reported in Lawyer's Co-op's *American Law Reports* includes evaluations and comments by a number of lawyers and/or legal editors.

Corpus juris secundum:
*Corpus Juris Secundum* is a legal encyclopedia published by the West Publishing Company. *Corpus Juris Secundum* is more difficult to read than other legal encyclopedias, but it is still very useful for detailed research, as it contains a large number of footnotes describing other sources of information.

Legal dictionaries:
*Legal dictionaries* are reference books that provide definitions, explain the origins of legal terms, and list the cases that led to the creation of a specific legal term.

Legal periodicals:
*Legal periodicals* are journals providing information related to a variety of different cases and legal issues. Legal periodicals analyze a number of different cases and offer expert opinions regarding the impact of those cases on the legal field.

Restatements of law:
*Restatements of Law* is a series of books published by the American Law Institute, in which legal experts explain the basic legal rules that apply to a variety of different legal fields. Each *Restatement of Law* offers a number of applications, examples, and explanations related to a single legal field or a specific legal topic.

Treatises:
*Treatises* are reference books that provide information related to a specific legal field or a specific legal topic. Treatises are written by experts in a particular area of law.

**Statutes**

The three main types of statutes are federal statutes, state statutes, and local ordinances. Federal statutes include any law established by the legislative branch of the federal government. A federal statute is typically published in the *United States Code* (U.S.C.) and is always published in the *Statutes at Large* (Stat.). State statutes

*Copyright © Mometrix Media. You have been licensed one copy of this document for personal use only. Any other reproduction or redistribution is strictly prohibited. All rights reserved.*

include any law established by the legislative branch of a state government. A state statute is typically published in an official publication released by the state and/or an unofficial publication published by a private company, such as West of Lawyer's Co-op. Local ordinances include any law established by a city or town government. Local ordinances are published, but the specific way that each city or town publishes their ordinances varies greatly from city to city and town to town.

### Bill:
A bill is a legal rule or regulation that has been proposed, but has not yet been passed into law. It is important to note that a bill has no legal weight until it passes.

### Slip law:
A slip law is a law that has been passed, but the law is not yet available with other laws in an official publication. A slip law is binding and on paper, but is unpublished and undistributed. It is important to note that a slip law carries the same weight as any other law.

### Session law:
A session law has been published in an official publication with other laws. In other words, a slip law becomes a session law once it is published with other slip laws. Session laws are recorded in chronological order.

### Statutory code:
A statutory code is a collection of session laws that are organized by topic.

### Annotation:
An annotation explains the law described in a statute, or expands on the information included in a statute by providing references to cases that may affect the interpretation or enforcement of the law established by the statute.

### Key number system:
The key number system is a statute organization system. Each topic is assigned a key number. The researcher looks up topics by their key numbers, instead of finding the topic in an alphabetical list.

### Official publication:
An official publication is any collection of statutes published and/or authorized by a federal, state, or local government.

### Unofficial publication:
An unofficial publication is any collection of statutes that is published by a private company such as West or Lawyer's Co-op, without the explicit authorization of the government.

Copyright © Mometrix Media. You have been licensed one copy of this document for personal use only. Any other reproduction or redistribution is strictly prohibited. All rights reserved.

## Court decision

A court decision is the final ruling that a judge and/or jury made in a particular case. Court decisions are an important part of case law because they can be used as precedent if certain conditions are met. However, it is important to note that court decisions often carry significantly more weight if they were made in the same jurisdiction as the case that the lawyer is attempting to prove. Note that a court may decide to dismiss a case, reverse the ruling that was made for a case, or take another similar action that ends a case. This is important to keep in mind because a decision that ends a case is also considered a court decision.

## Court opinion

A court opinion is the court's final comment on a case. Court opinions typically explain why the court made a particular decision in a particular case and describe the final statements that a judge made in a particular case.

## Concurring opinion

A concurring opinion is a type of appellate court opinion in which a single judge or a panel of judges agrees (concurs) with the original court's decision, but indicates the first court arrived at that decision for the wrong reason. The appellate court believes that the logic used by the deciding judge to arrive at the ruling is flawed, but the decision is still appropriate.

## Dissenting opinion

A dissenting opinion is a type of appellate court opinion in which a single judge or a panel of judges disagree with the court's decision and the logic behind that decision. The appellate court believes that a judge's original decision is inappropriate and unfounded.

## Majority opinion

A majority opinion is a type of appellate court opinion in which most, if not all, of the judges on the panel believe that the decision and the logic used to reach that decision are appropriate. This type of court opinion can be extremely useful to lawyers in some cases, as the opinion may be used as precedent if certain conditions are met. However, it is important to note that an appellate court can only issue one majority opinion per case.

## Per curiam opinion

A per curiam opinion is a type of appellate court opinion in which all of the judges on a panel or, in the case of an *en banc* opinion, all of the judges on the bench, issue a

Copyright © Mometrix Media. You have been licensed one copy of this document for personal use only. Any other reproduction or redistribution is strictly prohibited. All rights reserved.

single joint opinion. *Per curiam* opinions do not identify the specific judge who wrote the opinion, as the opinion is considered to be the opinion of the court, and not that of a specific judge.

## En banc opinion

An *en banc* opinion is more commonly referred to as an opinion issued *en banc*. It is a type of appellate court opinion in which all of the judges on the bench provide their comments on a particular case. *En banc* opinions typically occur in cases involving complicated legal issues, significant social issues, or rulings that contradict previous rulings. It is important to note that the judges involved in an *en banc* opinion do not necessarily have to agree with each others' assessments. As a result, an en banc opinion may actually refer to a number of different opinions, providing those opinions are issued by all of the judges on the bench and not just a specific panel of judges.

## Memorandum opinion

A memorandum opinion is an extremely short opinion issued by a court. Most memoranda opinions include a quick review of the court's decision and nothing else. A memorandum opinion cannot be used to establish precedent in most cases.

## Court record

A court record is an official report of all of the information related to a particular case. Court records are often lengthy because they cover different aspects of the case, including: Information related to the exhibits presented; motions made by the parties involved; any court orders issued; all pleas entered by the parties involved; and transcripts of the case.

## On the record

The phrase **on the record** refers to the decision of an appellate court to try a case based solely on the legal errors contained in a court record. The appellate court judges examine the court record exclusively to determine if the court that originally heard the case made a mistake in interpreting the law.

## Case report

There is a wide range of different information that will typically be included in a case report. However, most case reports contain:
1. A beginning caption that identifies the court, the groups involved, and the docket number of the case.
2. A middle portion indicating the date that the decision was made, identifying any other locations in which the record may be published, an explanation of

*Copyright © Mometrix Media. You have been licensed one copy of this document for personal use only. Any other reproduction or redistribution is strictly prohibited. All rights reserved.*

the legal issues addressed in the case, and a summary identifying the specifics of the case.
3. A closing statement indicating the court's opinion, any precedent that the case has set, an explanation of the logic behind the court's decision, additional comments of lesser importance that were made by the court, and the court's final decision.

## De novo

The Latin phrase *de novo* literally means "from the beginning" or "about making new". *De novo* refers to the decision of an appellate court to try a case as if the appellate court was the first court to hear that case. The appellate judge's approach a *de novo* case as completely new case, even though the case has already been heard by a lower court.

De novo on the record:
The phrase *de novo on the record* refers to the decision of an appellate court to try a case based primarily on the information contained in the record provided by the lower court. The parties involved in a case that is tried *de novo on the record* are prohibited from offering new evidence, but the appellate court will use the information in the record in order to determine the facts of the situation.

## Executive order

An executive order is given by the President of the United States or a state governor in emergency situations. An executive order directs an agency or a group of agencies to act in a certain way. Executive orders issued by the President are law when issued with an Act of Congress granting the president special discretionary powers, e.g., President Clinton's EO 13088 in June 1998 for the war in Kosovo. An example of an executive order applicable to one state was Governor Perdue's October 2007 EO to reduce Georgia's government water consumption during a drought.

## Interstate compact

An interstate compact is an executive action in which a pair or group of states' governors agree to recognize an interstate law addressing a specific issue concerning all of the states involved. For example, several states may establish an interstate compact regulating the transport of hazardous substances over state lines.

## Treaty

A treaty is an executive action in which two or more countries make an agreement to recognize an international law.

*Copyright © Mometrix Media. You have been licensed one copy of this document for personal use only. Any other reproduction or redistribution is strictly prohibited. All rights reserved.*

**Precedents**

There are three conditions that a case must meet to qualify for use as a precedent:
1. There must be a published court report of the case.
2. The case considered as precedent must be comparable (almost identical) to the case that the court is about to hear.
3. The case that is being considered as precedent must have been decided by a majority decision from a higher court than the court that is now hearing the case.

Note that a precedent will always carry more weight in the jurisdiction in which the precedent occurred. However, precedents from other jurisdictions may sometimes be useful in certain cases. Precedents established by the United States Supreme Court will always carry significant weight, regardless of the jurisdiction.

**Federal legal system**

The three main types of courts that report cases for the federal legal system are:
1. United States District Courts hear civil and criminal cases related to the violation of federal law, and usually use unofficial publications to report cases.
2. United States Courts of Appeal hear federal cases that have been decided in other federal courts, but are then appealed. Like U.S. District Courts, U.S. Courts of Appeals also use unofficial publications to report their cases.
3. United States Supreme Court hears cases that have been decided in a U.S. Court of Appeals or decided by a court that is recognized as the highest court in a particular state, which is typically a state supreme court, if certain conditions are met. The U.S. Supreme Court reports cases in official publications, including *United States Law Week* (U.S.L.W.), the *United States Supreme Court Bulletin*, and *United States Reports*, and unofficial publications, including the *Supreme Court Reporter* and the *Supreme Court Reporter, Lawyer's Edition*.

Specialty courts:
There are specialty courts that hear cases related to specific areas of law, which report cases for the federal legal system. These specialty courts include:
1. U.S. Bankruptcy Courts, which hear cases related to individuals or organizations filing bankruptcy. U.S. Bankruptcy Courts report decisions in the official *Bankruptcy Reporter*.
2. U.S. Claims Court, which hears cases related to claims brought against the U.S. government and reports them in an official publication published by the court itself, the *Records of the United States Court of Claims*, available through the National Archives at www.archives.gov.

*Copyright © Mometrix Media. You have been licensed one copy of this document for personal use only. Any other reproduction or redistribution is strictly prohibited. All rights reserved.*

3. U.S. Court of Appeals for the Armed Forces, which hears cases decided by a military court and subsequently appealed. Cases heard by the U.S. Court of Appeals for the Armed Forces are reported on its Web site, in LEXIS and WESTLAW, and the official West's *Military Justice Reporter* and *Military Justice Digest*, and McGraw-Hill's *Shepard's Military Justice Citations*.

## Advance sheets

An advance sheet is a collection of slip opinions that is published before the next case reporter for a federal court is published. Advance sheets are typically published in a loose-leaf or soft-cover book, in which the pages of the book are numbered in a similar way to the court's standard case reporter.

## Case reporter

A case reporter is a publication in which a court reports its cases, decisions, and opinions. Case reporters are typically published as a series of hardcover volumes that researchers use to find a particular case by name, or by statute, and/or by subject.

## Slip opinion

A slip opinion is a court opinion that is issued by a federal court immediately following the court's decision in a particular case. Slip opinions do not include headnotes and are usually not recorded in any particular order.

## Star paging

Star paging refers to a publishing practice in which a particular spot on a page is marked with an asterisk, star, or another similar mark and a page number to indicate that a change in the format has occurred. Star paging is an important practice for paralegals to know because certain case reporters, such as the *United States Reports*, have changed the way that they number the pages in their publications over time. As a result, the page that a particular case falls on may vary depending on the specific version of the publication that a paralegal uses for research. In order to prevent confusion, case reporters that are printed in multiple versions with significant differences in page numbering will use star paging to mark the spot in which the pages of another version of the publication begin and end.

## State legal systems

In most states, there are two types of courts that report cases for the state legal system: The State Court of Appeals and State Supreme Court. A State Court of Appeals hears a case decided in a lower court within the same state, but one or more parties involved in the case appealed the lower court's decision. A State Supreme

*Copyright © Mometrix Media. You have been licensed one copy of this document for personal use only. Any other reproduction or redistribution is strictly prohibited. All rights reserved.*

Court hears a case decided by the State Court of Appeals, but one or more parties involved in the case appealed the decision, so this is a second appeal. It is important to note that the specific publications that a state court uses to report its cases can vary greatly from state to state. Some states publish their case reports in official publications, while other states publish their case reports in unofficial publications. Certain states, notably California and New York, report cases from their lower state courts, in addition to the cases from their higher state courts.

## The *National Reporter System*

The *National Reporter System*, which is published by the West Publishing Company, is a collection of unofficial case reporters covering all cases decided at the state and federal level. The *National Reporter System* refers to a series of private publications that include case reports for cases decided in state and federal courts. The portion of the *National Reporter System* devoted to the state courts is divided into seven regional reporters. Each regional reporter covers the cases in a specific section of the United States. These regional reporters include the *Atlantic Reporter*, the North *Eastern Reporter*, the *North Western Reporter*, the *Pacific Reporter*, the *South Eastern Reporter*, the *South Western Reporter*, and the *Southern Reporter*. The portion of the *National Reporter System* devoted to the federal courts is split into a number of different reporters, such as the *Federal Reporter*, the *Supreme Court Reporter*, and the *Federal Supplement*.

## Case law from other jurisdictions

In most cases, the precedent or case law established in one jurisdiction will not carry much weight with a court in another jurisdiction. A foreign precedent may not be considered at all. However, there are some cases in which the precedent set in another jurisdiction may be useful. For example, if the current legal issue has never been addressed before within a jurisdiction, the foreign precedent may be considered. If the current legal issue questions a previous interpretation of the law, the foreign precedent may be considered. Note that the distance between the jurisdiction in which the case is heard and the jurisdiction in which the precedent was set affects the usefulness of the precedent. Precedents set in jurisdictions near the deciding jurisdiction carry more weight than precedents set in distant jurisdictions.

## *Research Skills*

### Citing appropriate legal authorities

The legal assistant may remember the name of a specific case similar to the present situation, or may have a citation or call number from a specific case related to a particular issue. The legal assistant searches the legal authorities alphabetically by name for that case by using the citation or finding a citation. However, if the legal

- 64 -

*Copyright © Mometrix Media. You have been licensed one copy of this document for personal use only. Any other reproduction or redistribution is strictly prohibited. All rights reserved.*

assistant only has the name of a case, he or she should attempt to find a citation by conducting a computer search, locating the case in *Shepard's Acts and Cases by Popular Name: Federal and State*, or by locating the case in a table of cases in a digest.

Often, a legal assistant may not have the name of a specific case, or a related citation, or a call number related to the case for which he or she is conducting research. The legal assistant searches legal authorities by legal issue for an appropriate match. This can usually be accomplished by using a digest or a general index to look up the legal issue. Useful resources include the *United States Supreme Court Digest,* the *American Digest System,* and the general index for the *United States Code*. They allow the legal assistant to locate the statutes relevant to a particular legal issue by topic.

## Search guides

Digest:
A digest is a search guide designed to help researchers locate cases based on the legal issues or topics. Digests are typically published by the company or organization that published the detailed case reporter. Digests include the case summaries provided in the headnotes of the actual case reporter. Digests are very useful in legal research because they are organized by topic rather than case; however, a digest is *only* a search guide and not a legal authority.

General index:
A general index is a search guide designed to help researchers locate statutes based on the legal issues or topics. General indices are included in every publication of a federal or state statutory code. Like digests, general indices are very useful in legal research because they are organized by topic rather than case, but it is important to note that a general index is *only* a search guide and not a legal authority.

The *American Digest System*:
The *American Digest System* is a series of digests published by the West Publishing Company. Each digest within the system contains a series of summaries from the headnotes of different case reports, organized by topic and key number. The digests in the *American Digest System* cover all of the cases reported in the federal and state courts by ten-year periods, so they are called decennials. A digest does not cover cases from a specific case reporter. Each digest is assigned a number based on the number of decades that passed between the time that the first volume of the digest was published and the time that the current volume of the digest was published. Note that there are two exceptions to this naming and numbering scheme:
1. The first volume of the digest is known as the *Century Digest.*
2. The current volume of the digest is always referred to as the *General Digest.*

Copyright © Mometrix Media. You have been licensed one copy of this document for personal use only. Any other reproduction or redistribution is strictly prohibited. All rights reserved.

TARP method:
The TARP Method is a technique publishers use to determine the key number assigned to a case. TARP is an acronym that refers to the four aspects of a case that the publisher looks at in order to choose the appropriate key number.
- **T**hing, which is the main topic, such as a car accident.
- **A**ction, which is the reason behind filing the legal action or the defense offered against the legal action.
- **R**elief, which refers to the plaintiff's objective for winning the case.
- **P**arties, which details the way that the parties involved in the case were related.

Legal databases:
A legal database is a computer program designed to help researchers quickly find cases or statutes related to a particular legal issue. On-line legal databases include up-to-date information related to the original rulings of each case, changes made to the decision of a case due to an appeal, the original wording of each statute, and/or the changes made to the wording of a particular statute. CD-ROM databases are soon stale dated. The two most widely used legal databases are LexisNexis, a product of the Mead Data Corporation, and WESTLAW, a product of the West Publishing Company.

*Advantages:* The three main advantages of using a legal database are:
1. Ease of access
2. Information control
3. Citation verification

Most legal databases are on-line, meaning legal researchers can access the information that they need from any computer connected to the Internet. Legal databases provide a large amount of information from a variety of different sources, so it is very easy for a legal researcher to find a lot of information in one location. The user creates parameters for the search, meaning the researcher instructs the database to ignore certain types of cases, statutes, or other types of information that are undesirable. Hence, the legal researcher controls the amount of information that he or she receives and prioritizes it. Finally, most legal databases include a list of citations or a software feature that can be used to double-check each citation that the researcher may need to use.

*Disadvantages:* A legal database can be a very useful tool for a legal researcher, but there are several disadvantages to using a legal database:
1. Legal databases contain so many cases and statutes that the researcher finds too much information if he/she does not define the parameters well. There is no way for the database to determine what is useful and what is not.
2. No legal databases are free. The major legal databases are quite expensive. Some law firms may be unable to afford the fees for a current database.

*Copyright © Mometrix Media. You have been licensed one copy of this document for personal use only. Any other reproduction or redistribution is strictly prohibited. All rights reserved.*

3. A legal database is just a search engine and may not list a case or statute if a search word or topic is not associated with that particular case or statute.

Loose-leaf services:
A loose-leaf service is offered by some legal publishers to provide hard copy updates that describe new cases, new statutes, or changes that occurred in a particular field of law recently. Each loose-leaf update consists of one or more hole-punched pages the user inserts into a binder. It is not as current as a Web-based service.

**Legal research process**

These are the steps that a legal assistant must follow during the legal research process:
1. Look at the facts of the situation and determine which are relevant to the case.
2. Determine the legal issues pertaining to the relevant facts.
3. Find the legal authorities related to those legal issues and determine which can be used to prove the lawyer's point.
4. Ensure each legal authority you use is up-to-date (no additional parallel citations).
5. Create a brief summarizing all the key points related to the case for each legal authority.
6. Ensure all of the information actually applies to the case and, if it does, create a memo to the attorney.

Citation:
A citation is a brief note identifying the legal authority that provided the information the publisher or legal researcher used in a legal document. A citation uses short forms for administrative laws, cases, constitutions, procedural rules, and statutes so that they take up the minimum amount of space.

Shepard's citations:
*Shepard's Citations* is published by Shepard's/McGraw-Hill Publishing. It lists citations for every case reported within the United States. *Shepard's Citations* can be extremely helpful for a researcher attempting to locate a particular case.

Shepardizing:
Shepardizing means the legal researcher uses *Shepard's Citations* to determine if a case has been overturned on appeal, has had its decision modified, has been reaffirmed by another case, or has been overruled by another decision.

Updating:
Updating refers to a practice in which the researcher determines if the legal implications of a case or statute have changed.

Copyright © Mometrix Media. You have been licensed one copy of this document for personal use only. Any other reproduction or redistribution is strictly prohibited. All rights reserved.

**Proper citation**

An Amendment to the U.S. Constitution:
A citation for an amendment to the U.S. constitution should include the abbreviation *U.S. Const.,* and the abbreviation *amend,* followed by the amendment number, the applicable section, and the exact clause in which the information that the citation is referencing is found. For example, the second clause of the first section of the first amendment to the U.S. constitution is cited as U.S. Const. amend. I, §1, cl. 2.

An Article in the U.S. Constitution:
A citation for an article in the U.S. Constitution should include the abbreviation *U.S. Const.*, and the abbreviation *art.*, followed by the article number, the applicable section, and the exact clause in which the information that the citation is referencing can be found. For example, the first clause of the second section of the third article of the Constitution is cited as U.S. Const. art. III, §2, cl. 1

Federal procedural rule:
A citation for a federal procedural rule must include the type of federal rule that the citation is referencing, and the abbreviation *P.*, followed by the procedural rule number. For example, the 15th rule of the Federal rules of Criminal Procedure is cited as Fed. R. Crim. P. 15. With this format in mind, it is important to note that each type of federal rule has its own abbreviation and the appropriate abbreviation must appear within the citation. The four abbreviations for federal procedural rules are *Fed. R. App.* for the Federal Rules of Appellate Procedure, *Fed. R. Civ.* for the Federal Rules of Civil Procedure, *Fed. R. Crim.* for the Federal Rules of Criminal Procedure, and *Fed. R. Evid.* for the Federal Rules of Evidence.

Court case:
A citation for a court case should include the:
1. Case name.
2. Volume number.
3. Name of the publication in which the case was reported.
4. Page that the case first appears on.
5. Name of the court that issued the decision in the case (unless the publication in which the case was reported only reports cases for one court).
6. Year in which the court issued a decision for that case.

For example, if a case known as Wallace versus Doe was decided by the Massachusetts Supreme Judicial Court in 2001 and published in the *North Eastern Reporter*, cite the case as Wallace v. Doe, 442 N.E. 2d 355 (Mass. 2001). Note that you may need to include additional information in a citation, known as subsequent history, if the decision in the case has been reversed, modified on appeal, or is affected by some other legal action.

*Copyright © Mometrix Media. You have been licensed one copy of this document for personal use only. Any other reproduction or redistribution is strictly prohibited. All rights reserved.*

Court case with subsequent history:

A citation for a court case with a subsequent history uses the same format as the original case, except the subsequent history appears after the year. This means that a citation for a court case with a subsequent history should include the:

1. Case name.
2. Volume number.
3. Name of the publication in which the case was reported.
4. Page that the case first appears on.
5. Name of the court that issued the decision in the case (unless the publication in which the case was reported only reports cases for one court).
6. Year in which the court issued a decision for that case.
7. Subsequent history.

For example, if a case known as Wallace versus Doe was decided by the Massachusetts Supreme Judicial Court in 2001, published in the *North Eastern Reporter*, and then reversed by the United States Supreme Court, cite it as Wallace v. Doe, 442 N.E. 2d 355 (Mass. 2001) rev. U.S. 622 (2003).

An Administrative Law from the *Code of Federal Regulations:*

A citation for an administrative law from the *Code of Federal Regulations* must include the chapter number, the abbreviation C.F.R., the section number, and the year that the administrative law was first published. For example, section 42.7 of the 20th chapter of the *Code of Federal Regulations* is cited as 20 C.F.R. § 42.7 (1989).

An Administrative Law from the *Federal Register:*

A citation for an administrative law from the *Federal Register* must include the volume number, the abbreviation Fed. Reg., the page number that the administrative law first appears on, and the year the administrative law was first published. For example, an administrative law on page 4,442 of the 45th volume of the *Federal Register* is cited as 45 Fed. Reg. 4,442 (1980).

A Statute from the *Statutes at Large:*

A citation for an entry in the *Statues at Large* must include the act's name, and the abbreviation *Pub. L.*, followed by the statute's public law number, the volume number of the *Statutes at Large* in which the statute appears, the abbreviation *Stat.*, the page number that the statute first appears on, and the year that the statute was passed into law. For example, a statute known as the Water Protection Act passed as Public Law 90-215 in 1983 appearing on page 550 of the 79th volume of the Statutes at Large is cited as Water Protection Act, Pub. L. 90-215, 79 Stat. 550 (1983).

A Statute from the *United States Code:*

A citation for a statute from the *United States Code* must include the title number of the code, the abbreviation *U.S.C.*, the section number that the statute appears in, and the date that the code in which the statute appears was most recently published.

*Copyright © Mometrix Media. You have been licensed one copy of this document for personal use only. Any other reproduction or redistribution is strictly prohibited. All rights reserved.*

For example, a statute that appears in section 4 of the 22nd volume of the *United States Code* is written as 22 U.S.C. §4 (2000).

<u>*American Law Report*</u>:
A citation for an *American Law Report* entry must include the author's first and last name, the term *Annotation*, the title of the annotated report, the volume number of the *American Law Report* publication in which the annotated report appears, the abbreviation *A.L.R.*, followed by an abbreviation of the name of the series, the page number that the annotated report first appears on, and the year that the annotated report was published. For example, an American Law Report entitled Probable Cause versus Illegal Search and Seizure written by Jacob Myers in 2001, which appeared on page 242 of the 90th volume of the American Law Report's Federal Series, is cited as Jacob Myers, Annotation, <u>Probable Cause vs. Illegal Search and Seizure,</u> 90 A.L.R. Fed. 242 (2001).

<u>Legal articles:</u>
A citation for a legal article must include the author's first and last names, the type of article if the article was written by a student, the article's title, the volume number of the legal periodical in which the article appears, an abbreviation of the name of the legal periodical in which the article appears, the page number on which the article first appears, and the year that the article was published. For example, a legal article entitled Medical Malpractice written by Christina White as a comment on the legal issue discussed on page 142 in the 25th volume of the *Texas Law Review* in 1997 is cited as Christina White, Comment, <u>Medical Malpractice,</u> 25 Tex. L. Rev. 142 (1997).

<u>Legal dictionary:</u>
A citation for a legal dictionary must include the title of the dictionary, the page that the term appears on, the edition of the dictionary in which the term appears, and the year in which the dictionary was published. For example, a reference to a term appearing on page 225 of the 3rd edition of The Reliable Law Dictionary that was published in 1999 is cited as The Reliable Law Dictionary 225 (3rd ed. 1999). Note that the title of a legal dictionary should never be abbreviated, underlined, or italicized within a citation. This means that the title of the dictionary in the above example should always be written as The Reliable Law Dictionary and not as Rel. L. Dict., <u>The Reliable Law Dictionary,</u> or *The Reliable Law Dictionary*.

<u>Legal encyclopedia:</u>
A citation for a legal encyclopedia must include the volume number of the encyclopedia in which the article appears, an abbreviation for the name of the encyclopedia, the title of the article, the section number, the page number of the article if only part of the section is being cited, and the date that the encyclopedia with the article was published. For example, cite an article on child support appearing in section 37 of the 100th volume of *American Jurisprudence*, Second Series, if only page 323 is relevant, published in 1990 as 100 Am. Jur. 2d <u>Child</u>

*Copyright © Mometrix Media. You have been licensed one copy of this document for personal use only. Any other reproduction or redistribution is strictly prohibited. All rights reserved.*

Support § 37, 323 (1990.). However, cite the article in this example as 100 Am. Jur. 2d Child Support §37 (1990.) *if the entire section is being cited as relevant.*

**Parallel citation**

A parallel citation is not always required for a case reported in more than one legal authority, but it is required in certain jurisdictions. Some states require parallel citations to be included in all documents identifying a case reported in more than one location. Federal courts do not typically require parallel citations and they are not required in every state. Most of the states that require parallel citations specify they are only required if the document identifies a case that originated within that state. Paralegals must know the state and local procedural rules for citing cases in the specific jurisdiction in which they work.

Information included:
A parallel citation must identify each publication in which the case appears, so include the:
1. Case name.
2. Volume number of the first publication.
3. Name of the first publication in which the case was reported.
4. Page that the case first appears on in the first publication.
5. Volume number of the second publication.
6. Name of the second publication.
7. Page that the case first appears on in the second publication.
8. Name of the court that issued the decision (unless one of the publications only reports cases for one court.
9. Year in which the court decided the case.

For example, if a case known as Williams versus Allen was decided by the Ohio Supreme Court in 2002 and published in the case reporter for the Ohio Supreme Court and the *North Eastern Reporter*, cite the case as Williams v. Allen, 255 Ohio 124, 455 N.E. 2d 392 (2002).

**Citation signal**

A citation signal is a single word or a short phrase that appears before a citation in a brief, memo, or other legal document. Each word or phrase in the signal indicates the reason why the author asks the reader to look at a particular legal authority. The authority can be used to contradict a particular point, directly state a particular point, prove a particular point, provide background information, or to perform another function. A citation signal can apply to more than one citation, but the citations must appear in a certain order. A series of citations within a single citation signal should appear in the following order: U.S. Constitution citations, federal statute citations, federal procedural rule citations, federal case citations, state case

*Copyright © Mometrix Media. You have been licensed one copy of this document for personal use only. Any other reproduction or redistribution is strictly prohibited. All rights reserved.*

citations, administrative law citations, law review article citations, annotation citations, legal encyclopedia citations, and finally law dictionary citations.

## Citation terms

*Infra:* The Latin term *infra* literally means below or after. *Infra* is used in a brief, memo, or other legal document to notify the reader that a full citation will appear somewhere below the short citation in which *infra* appears.

*Parallel Citation:* A parallel citation is a brief note identifying a group of publications in which a particular case can be found. A parallel citation indicates a case was reported in more than one publication.

*Supra:* The Latin term *supra* literally means above or earlier, but is interpreted as see above. The term *supra* is used in a brief, memo, or other legal document to notify the reader that a full citation appears somewhere above the short citation in which *supra* appears. Do not use *supra* in a short citation if the full citation refers to a case, a constitution, or a statute.

*Contra:* The Latin term *contra* literally means against. *Contra* indicates that the legal authority mentioned in a citation contradicts the point another party is attempting to make.

*Cf.:* Cf. is an abbreviation for the Latin term *confer*, which literally means compare. Cf. indicates that the legal authority mentioned in a citation doesn't necessarily prove the document author's point, but it makes a comparable point that supports the document author's point.

*See:* See indicates that a legal authority establishes the same point as the document author, but it does not state that point in the same way.

*See, e.g.:* See, e.g., indicates that the legal authority establishes the same point as the document's author, but there also other legal authorities that make the same point as well.

*See generally:* See generally indicates that a legal authority offers background information to help the reader understand the point the document's author is attempting to make.

*Copyright © Mometrix Media. You have been licensed one copy of this document for personal use only. Any other reproduction or redistribution is strictly prohibited. All rights reserved.*

# Judgment and Analytical Ability

## Comprehension of Data

### Analytical Ability

Where legal assistants are concerned, analytical ability refers to the capability of classifying information. The legal assistant screens information by asking:
- Is it related to this particular case?
- Is it relevant to the lawyer's argument?
- Is it true and legal?
- How can it be logically arranged (in order of importance, chronologically, alphabetically, by jurisdiction, or in some other way)?
- Is it easy or difficult for the lawyer to understand and present?

Extraneous information is excluded or kept in a miscellaneous file if it has bearing on a similar case.

## Application of Knowledge

### Judgment

Judgment is decision-making ability. The legal assistant determines the best option from a group of possible actions, usually to achieve a certain outcome. For example, a legal assistant exercises judgment when deciding the best way to complete a project for a particular case, so the filing deadline is met.

### Decision-making

Technique:
This is the basic four-step decision-making technique a paralegal uses when exercising good judgment:
1. Gather as much information as possible from as many reliable sources as possible.
2. List the advantages and disadvantages of each choice.
3. Compare each choice with its counterparts.
4. Identify the best available option for the specific situation.

The four steps make arriving at a difficult decision easier. Pay special attention to the resources that each option will use. Ask yourself if each option furthers your objective. Bear in mind the length of time that the option will take to perform. The option you choose must be practical, effective, legal, within budget, and within schedule.

Copyright © Mometrix Media. You have been licensed one copy of this document for personal use only. Any other reproduction or redistribution is strictly prohibited. All rights reserved.

Ethics:
Legal assistants are expected to make ethical decisions regardless of the situation. The legal assistant must have ready access to an ethical code, on-line or in book format. The legal assistant must know the ethical rules that apply to a given situation. There may be situations in which the legal assistant cannot choose an option, even though it appears logical and supports the desired outcome with the fewest resources possible, because the option violates an ethical rule. This means that in order for a legal assistant to make effective decisions, he or she must consider the ethical implications of each choice before he or she makes a decision.

Daily decisions:
The legal assistant is commonly be required to decide:
- Whether he/she has the **authority** to carry out a task, or if it requires a lawyer.
- The best way to carry out a task to meet the **objective.**
- Whether or not a particular action is **ethical.**
- If the resources required to complete a particular task are within **budget.**
- How to stay within **schedule.**
- Which **legal procedures** apply in various situations.

These are not the only types of decisions that a legal assistant may be required to make. They are general guidelines only, as there are a vast number of situations in which a legal assistant may be required to make a decision.

**Reasoning**

Analogical Reasoning:
The process by which the paralegal makes a decision for a present situation based on his/her experience with a similar situation in the past. The paralegal compares two or more particulars. It is the simplest, most common reasoning method. However, analogical reasoning presents the most opportunity for the paralegal to make an error.

Deductive Reasoning:
The process by which the paralegal takes general laws or principles and tries to apply them to a particular situation. The paralegal tries to determine cause and effect based on all available information.

Stare Decisis:
Latin for 'to stand by that which is decided'. The principle of stare decisis means the courts should decide cases based on precedent (historical cases). Stare decisis was intended to provide consistency. The court would render the same decision in two cases involving similar situations, but two different decisions in two cases involving

- 74 -

*Copyright © Mometrix Media. You have been licensed one copy of this document for personal use only. Any other reproduction or redistribution is strictly prohibited. All rights reserved.*

different situations. However, stare decisis is routinely overturned by appeals, new legislation, Supreme Court decisions, and en banc decisions.

Reasoning process:
To complete an analogy that is missing a term, follow these three steps:

1. Look at the two related terms and try to determine their relationship to each other. For example, take the analogy *Pirate is to ship as __ is to __*. A pirate *travels* in a ship.
2. Look at each available option. Determine their relationship to each other. Option 1 is *chef* and *pan*. Option 2 is *driver* and *racecar*.
3. Choose the option with the two terms that have the same relationship as the terms in the analogy. A driver *travels* in a racecar. Although a pirate uses a ship and a chef uses a pan, the closest analogy is *Pirate is to ship as driver is to racecar*.

Relationships in analogies:
Analogies can contain relationships that define another term. Consider the analogy *Prevent is to stop* as an analogy that defines. Analogies can indicate a type. Consider the analogy *Tiger is to cat* as an analogy of type. Analogies can contain opposite relationships, as in the analogy *Hot is to cold*. Analogies can include synonyms (words that mean the same). Consider the analogy *Ebony is to black* as a synonymous analogy. An analogy can include a part of a whole, as in *Hand is to body*. Analogies may include a second term that is the extreme of the first term, as in *Frigid is to cold*. An analogy can include an object and its function, as in *Keyboard is to typing*. An analogy can indicate a lack or absence, as in *Cadaver is to life*. An analogy can signal something, as in *Sunset is to night*. An analogy can contain a locator term, as in *Hospital is to doctor*.

*Technique to determine relationship:* There are a number of different techniques to determine the relationship between two terms in an analogy. Here is a simple and effective technique:
Place each of the terms into a sentence that describes how the first term is related to the second term. Determine the type of relationship, based on whether the sentence makes sense or not. For example, to determine the relationship in the analogy *Night is to day*, try:

1.    Night is a *type* of day.
2.    Night is the *same as* day.
3.    Night *defines* day.
4.    Night is the *opposite* of day.

The terms do not make sense in the first 3 sentences, so it is safe to assume that night is not related to day in these ways. However, sentence 4 makes sense, so it is safe to assume that the terms are opposites.

*Copyright © Mometrix Media. You have been licensed one copy of this document for personal use only. Any other reproduction or redistribution is strictly prohibited. All rights reserved.*

**Deductive logic**

Avoid these two practices when using deductive logic to arrive at a conclusion:
1. Do not make assumptions.
2. Do not read the information too quickly.

Both of these practices lead you to make the wrong deduction. Assumptions based on stereotypes or on unrelated information may make your conclusion *appear* logical, even though the conclusion really can't be logically drawn from the information that is available. For example:

*Premise 1:* If New York City is the capital of New York State, then it is in New York State.
*Premise 2:* New York City is in New York State.
*Conclusion:* New York City is the capital of New York State.

This conclusion sounds plausible but is a **deductive fallacy**, because *Albany* is actually the capital of New York State. The two premises of the above deductive argument appeared to provide support for a true conclusion but do not, so this is **fallacious reasoning**. Avoid making assumptions based on unverified facts. Read all the information carefully to avoid misunderstanding long documents with difficult technical structure.

Determining a correct conclusion:
These are the six steps to take to determine if a conclusion is correct, based on the information that is available:
1. Determine which information is relevant and which information is irrelevant.
2. Carefully read all of the information that is relevant to the conclusion.
3. Ignore irrelevant information.
4. Determine whether each piece of relevant information supports or contradicts the conclusion.
5. If any of the information contradicts or disproves the conclusion, assume that the conclusion is incorrect.
6. If all of the information appears to support the conclusion and the conclusion logically follows the information that is available, assume that the conclusion is probably correct.

## Evaluating and Categorizing Data

**Factual Conflicts**

A factual conflict is a situation in which two pieces of information contradict each other. For example, Witness #1 testifies, "The thief who robbed the jewelry store last night was a tall man with black hair." Witness #2 testifies, "The thief who robbed the jewelry store last night was a tall man with blond hair." There is a factual conflict because both statements cannot be true.

Copyright © Mometrix Media. You have been licensed one copy of this document for personal use only. Any other reproduction or redistribution is strictly prohibited. All rights reserved.

## Factual Gaps

A factual gap is a situation in which an important piece of information is missing. For example, your client states, "I left the jewelry store at around 6:30 p.m. and then I went home around 10:30 p.m." You realize there is a factual gap because it is unclear if it took your client four hours to get home, or if he did something else during the four-hour period after leaving the store.

Copyright © Mometrix Media. You have been licensed one copy of this document for personal use only. Any other reproduction or redistribution is strictly prohibited. All rights reserved.

# Organizing Data and Findings

## Creating an abstract

The specific process that a legal assistant follows to create an abstract varies greatly from situation to situation and from firm to firm. However, here are the standard steps that a legal assistant should always follow when writing an abstract:

1. Determine which format is required for the abstract. Consider the type of information to be abstracted, the reason for the abstract, and the requirements set by the firm or the lawyer in charge of the case.
2. Develop a system for filing abstracts, if a system is not already in place. This will make it much easier to retrieve the information later.
3. Create the abstract by writing down any essential information and avoiding any nonessential information.

## Full case brief

Begin your full case brief with a statement. Name the case. Cite the legal authorities you relied upon. List any relevant precedents. List the courts that rendered decisions in the case. Give a court history describing the major actions that occurred during the court process for that case, and relevant context. State the results of a jury vote and any mandated decisions. List the issues the court must now decide. Then provide a brief **summary** of the facts of the case (a brief explanation of what happened). List the legal issues the court addressed, each court's decision, and the laws or legal grounds on which each court based its decision. Finally, explain the logic that each court used to make its decision (how it justified the ruling). List all concurrent and dissenting opinions.

Copyright © Mometrix Media. You have been licensed one copy of this document for personal use only. Any other reproduction or redistribution is strictly prohibited. All rights reserved.

## Sample questions

**Determine the option that completes the analogy *5 is to 25 as __ is to __.* Explain your reasoning.**
- A. 2 : 8
- B. 1 : 5
- C. 5 : 10
- D. 25 : 5

Option B is correct; *1* and *5* correctly complete the analogy. The analogy asks you to find a pair of terms with the same relationship that the number 5 has with the number 25. Since 5 is one-fifth of 25, the correct answer must have a second term that is five times greater than the first term. Option A is incorrect because it offers a second term that is 4 times the first term. Option C is incorrect because it offers a second term that is twice as large as the first term. Option D has the inverse relationship; 25 is 5 times 5.

**Determine the option that completes the analogy *Lawyer is to law as __ is to __.* Explain your reasoning.**
- A. doctor : medicine
- B. pharmacist : lab coat
- C. carpenter : hammer
- D. dehydrated: water

Option A is correct; *doctor* and *medicine* correctly complete the analogy. The analogy asks you to find a pair of terms with the same relationship that a lawyer has with the law. Since a lawyer practices law, the correct answer must indicate the relationship between a *profession* and a *practice*. Option B is incorrect because a pharmacist wears a lab coat, but a pharmacist does not practice sewing lab coats. Option C is incorrect because a carpenter may use a hammer, but a carpenter does not practice manufacturing hammers. Option D is incorrect because it indicates what someone who is dehydrated might want, instead of describing the relationship between a profession and what the profession practices.

**Determine the option that completes the analogy *Lion is to Feline as __ is to __.* Explain your reasoning.**
- A. dog : cat
- B. gorilla : animal
- C. wolf : canine
- D. monkey : human

Option C is correct; *wolf* and *canine* correctly complete the analogy. The analogy asks you to find a pair of terms with the same relationship that a lion has with the feline family. Since a lion is part of the feline family, the correct answer must indicate the relationship between a *particular animal* and the *family* to which it

- 79 -

*Copyright © Mometrix Media. You have been licensed one copy of this document for personal use only.*
*Any other reproduction or redistribution is strictly prohibited. All rights reserved.*

belongs. Option A is incorrect because dogs are canines, not felines. Option B is not the best answer because both gorillas and lions are part of the animal kingdom. The analogy describes a *specific* relationship, while Option B describes a *broad* relationship. Option D is incorrect because it describes two animals in the same phylum.

**Explain why the following deduction is true or is an untrue deductive fallacy.**

*Premise 1:* Most of the people at the office dress up for Halloween.
*Premise 2:* Danielle works at the office.
*Conclusion:* Danielle dresses up for Halloween.

It is illogical to conclude that *Danielle dresses up for Halloween* based solely on the information provided. Premise 1 states *most* of the people at the office dress up for Halloween. Most does not mean *all*—there are exceptions. Premise 2 states Danielle works at the office, but she might be one of the exceptions and not in the majority. Therefore, the conclusion, *Danielle dresses up for Halloween*, is a deductive fallacy. It is impossible to determine whether Danielle dresses up on Halloween from the scant information that is provided. It is fair to say it is *likely* that Danielle dresses up, but she may not.

**Explain why the above deduction is true or is an untrue deductive fallacy.**

*Premise 1:* The secretary is responsible for stocking the office supplies.
*Premise 2:* Hailey is the secretary for the office.
*Conclusion:* Hailey is responsible for keeping the office's supply cabinet stocked.

It is logical to conclude that Hailey is responsible for keeping the office's supply cabinet stocked, because both premises are relevant to determining the person who is responsible for stocking the supply cabinet, and both premises appear to support this conclusion. The secretary is responsible for stocking the office supplies, so the person who is the secretary for the office would be responsible for keeping the supply cabinet stocked. Hailey is the secretary for the office, so it is logical to conclude that Hailey is the person responsible for keeping the supply cabinet stocked. The first statement makes it clear that the secretary is responsible for stocking the cabinet and the second statement makes it clear that Hailey is the secretary. The conclusion is logically true.

**Explain why the above deduction is true or is an untrue deductive fallacy.**

*Premise 1:* Teachers must like kids.
*Premise 2:* Jay likes kids.
*Conclusion:* Jay is a teacher.

Copyright © Mometrix Media. You have been licensed one copy of this document for personal use only. Any other reproduction or redistribution is strictly prohibited. All rights reserved.

It is illogical to conclude that Jay is a teacher, based solely on the information that is provided. It is not necessarily true that teachers must like kids. For example, teachers may accept teaching because there are no other jobs, or they may like some kids and not others. Premise 2 is irrelevant to the conclusion. It is not safe to assume that Jay is a teacher simply because Jay happens to like kids. Jay could be a member of many other professions that work with children, like a neonatal nurse, or a pediatrician, or a daycare provider, or a clown. The conclusion is false. The deduction is fallacious. It is fair to conclude that *Jay might be a teacher*, or even, *Jay might make a good teacher*. However, it is not possible to logically conclude that Jay is a teacher from the information that is provided.

Copyright © Mometrix Media. You have been licensed one copy of this document for personal use only. Any other reproduction or redistribution is strictly prohibited. All rights reserved.

# Substantive Law

## American Legal System

**Law**

The Law is a collection of regulations and legal concepts established by government, courts, and other legal authorities to ensure the continued functioning of a community. The individual laws that make up the Law must be enforceable through some form of judicial action.

Public Law:
Public law is the way that the government interacts with the community and regulates it. Public law typically includes constitutional law, administrative law, and criminal law.

Private Law:
Private law is the regulations governing the way private citizens interact with each other. Public law typically includes civil law, commercial law, corporate law, and labor law.

**Rights**

A right is a legal claim, entitlement, ownership or interest, or an ethical or moral standard (rectitude). Rights established by a law are known as legal rights. Rights established by a moral or ethical standard are known as natural rights. There must be a specific duty associated with a right in order for that right to be enforced. If a person has a right, then someone else owes him/her a duty.

**Duties**

A duty is legal obligation, usually a task an individual is required to perform due to a law, an ethical standard, or a moral standard. Duties that are established by a law are often referred to as legal duties. Duties established by a moral or ethical standard are often referred to as natural duties. A duty must exist in order for a right to be enforced. Sometimes, duty refers to an import/export tax.

**Legal Positivism**

Legal positivism is a type of legal logic used in creating and/or interpreting law, in which a legal issue is decided based solely on the law related to that legal issue. However, it is important to note that legal positivism also establishes that a law should only be applied if it was passed using the same process used to pass any

Copyright © Mometrix Media. You have been licensed one copy of this document for personal use only. Any other reproduction or redistribution is strictly prohibited. All rights reserved.

other law. Legal positivism ignores the ethical or moral implications of a law and focuses on whether the process used to pass that law was fair and reasonable or not.

## Legal Realism

Legal realism is a type of legal logic used in creating and/or interpreting law, in which a legal issue is decided based on what a reasonable person would do if he or she was in the same situation as the individual or group involved in the legal issue. Legal realism establishes that the interpretation of law should be based on what a reasonable person would do in the same situation.

## Natural Law

Natural law is a type of legal logic used in creating and/or interpreting law, in which a legal issue is decided based on how it affects the rights of other people. The individual's right to choose does not prohibit another individual from exercising his or her right to do as he or she chooses.

## Sociological Jurisprudence

Sociological Jurisprudence is a type of legal logic used in creating and/or interpreting law, in which a legal issue is decided based on how it affects society as a whole. Sociological jurisprudence is based on the idea that society decides whether a particular action is right or not, so the interpretation of law should be based on the same logic that a society uses as a whole.

## Crime

The three main types of crimes that an individual or group can commit are a felony, a misdemeanor, and treason. A **felony** is any crime in which an individual or a group could receive the death penalty or a prison sentence of more than 364 days for committing the crime. Crimes that are considered felonies include arson, burglary, embezzlement, fraud, kidnapping, murder, robbery, and rape. A misdemeanor is any crime in which an individual could be fined or could receive a prison sentence of no more than 364 days for committing the crime. Crimes that are considered **misdemeanors** include prostitution, public intoxication, trespassing, and vandalism. Finally, **treason** refers to any crime in which an individual aids an enemy of the country or attempts to take control of the government through coercion or force. Treason is punishable by death.

## Contract

A contract is a written or verbal agreement establishing a specific set of responsibilities for each party to it. A contract is legally binding unless it contains illegal terms that are unenforceable, such as an agreement to commit murder. Any

Copyright © Mometrix Media. You have been licensed one copy of this document for personal use only. Any other reproduction or redistribution is strictly prohibited. All rights reserved.

party involved in a legal contract faces civil penalties for failing to uphold the agreement.

## Equitable Remedy

An equitable remedy is an action that a court orders an individual or group to perform to rectify damages and/or legal issues that the individual or group caused. Equitable remedies are ordered as part of the court's decision in a civil suit.

## Legal Remedy

A legal remedy is a payment that a court orders an individual or group to make as compensation to the opposing party for the damage and/or legal issues that the individual or group caused. Legal remedies are ordered as part of the court's decision in a civil suit.

## Tort

The three types of torts that an individual or group can commit are an intentional tort, a tort of strict liability, and an unintentional tort. An **intentional tort** is a wrongful act in which an individual deliberately performs an action that causes harm to another or a group. The wrongdoer realizes his/her actions will cause harm or are likely to cause harm. A **tort of strict liability** is a wrongful act in which an individual or a group fails to live up to their legal or moral obligations, even though the individual or group made every effort to do so. Finally, an **unintentional tort** is a wrongful act in which an individual does not deliberately cause harm to another individual or group, but harm is still caused as a result of his or her actions or the lack thereof.

## Separation of powers

The separation of powers is based on the idea that the powers of the government should be divided so that no single individual or group has the power to control the entire government. This is one of the fundamental concepts established by the United States Constitution, which divides the government into three branches: Legislative, judicial, and executive. The **legislative branch** has the authority to control the government's money, to establish law, and to declare war. The **judicial branch** has the authority to overturn laws deemed unconstitutional, to try cases, and to interpret and apply law. The **executive branch** has the authority to enforce the law, to veto laws, and to control the direct actions of the army.

## Administrative powers

The two administrative powers granted to administrative agencies are quasi-legislative powers and quasi-judicial powers. **Quasi-legislative powers** allow an

Copyright © Mometrix Media. You have been licensed one copy of this document for personal use only. Any other reproduction or redistribution is strictly prohibited. All rights reserved.

administrative agency to create the rules and regulations that help define the laws established by a particular type of statute in more specific terms. Each of the rules and regulations created by an administrative agency must be related to the specific area of law that it was assigned to oversee. **Quasi-judicial powers** allow an administrative agency to interpret and apply the rules and regulations established by the agency, to enforce the rules and regulations, and to conduct investigations of suspected violations of the rules and regulations.

## Administrative Procedure Act

The Administrative Procedure Act (APA) was passed in 1946. APA prevents administrative agencies from abusing their quasi-legislative and quasi-judicial powers. APA establishes that the decisions, rules, and regulations of an administrative agency may be reviewed and/or appealed to a federal court. However, the appellant of an administrative agency's decision, rule, or regulation must exhaust all legal options offered by the administrative agency itself before turning to the federal court. APA also establishes standards for administrative agencies. APA specifically requires an administrative agency to inform the public of the agency's, purpose, rules, regulations and procedures. APA requires agencies to involve the public in its quasi-legislative actions.

## National Conference of Commissioners on Uniform State Laws

The National Conference of Commissioners on Uniform State Laws is a non-profit association formed in 1915. NCCUSL established interstate laws simplify trade between states. Prior to 1915, each state had the authority to establish its own laws, which means laws for specific entities vary drastically from state to state. The laws established by the NCCUSL, more commonly known as **uniform laws**, are extremely useful because they prevent problems that arise from drastically different regulations in neighboring states. Uniform laws accomplish this by ensuring each state regulates the activities of entities (individuals and businesses) in a standardized fashion. However, it is important to note that a state is not required to adhere to a law or uniform code unless the state chooses to adopt that code.

## Common law and federal court decisions

A decision issued by a federal court can have a large impact on the common law in a particular jurisdiction. Many state courts consider federal court decisions as precedent in their decision-making. However, even though the decision of a federal court may affect the common law in a particular jurisdiction, it is important to remember that *common law does not affect federal court decisions*. Federal courts are expected to make their decisions based on federal rules and regulations, instead of basing their decisions on decisions previously made at the state or federal level (precedent). As a result, each federal case must be decided based on the legal issue at hand and the specific federal regulations that can be applied to that specific issue.

*Copyright © Mometrix Media. You have been licensed one copy of this document for personal use only. Any other reproduction or redistribution is strictly prohibited. All rights reserved.*

## United States Constitution

Effect on US legal system:
The United States Constitution is the foundation for the United States legal system in three main ways:
1. The U.S. Constitution identifies the specific powers granted to the federal government. These federal powers are described in the first three articles of the Constitution.
2. The U.S. Constitution describes the specific powers that state governments are prohibited from exercising. Most of the powers that state governments cannot use are reserved for the federal government by Article VI of the U.S. Constitution.
3. The U.S. Constitution describes the specific rights that the citizens of the United States are granted. These rights are described primarily in the first ten amendments to the Constitution, which are known as the Bill of Rights.

Limit on powers of state government:
The two ways that the United States Constitution limits states' powers are through the principle of federalism and the principle of pre-emption. **The principle of federalism** establishes that federal law must take precedence over state law if there is a direct conflict. If a legal issue is covered by both state and federal law, then the federal law is applied first if the laws disagree. This is important because you may deal with cases in which a state law is significantly different from a federal law. Remember that federal law always takes precedence. **The principle of preemption** establishes that there are certain situations in which the federal government can prevent a state government or a private citizen from taking an action that would interfere with an action that the federal government intends to take or has taken. For example, the federal government may choose to regulate a specific industry in the national interest and prohibit the state governments from passing laws related to that industry.

**Powers of state government**

The two major powers of every state government are the authority to self-regulate and the authority to police their own state. **The authority to self-regulate** allows a state government to create its own rules and regulations, providing they only apply to individuals or actions taken within the state itself. The laws passed by a state or local government may be reviewed and removed by the U.S. Supreme Court if the rule or regulation is determined to be unconstitutional. The state government's authority to police the state is known as **police power**, and allows it to establish and enforce rules, regulations, and enforcement procedures that protect the health, safety, and welfare of the individuals within the state.

Copyright © Mometrix Media. You have been licensed one copy of this document for personal use only. Any other reproduction or redistribution is strictly prohibited. All rights reserved.

## Articles of the United States Constitution

First article:

The first article of the United States Constitution establishes the **legislative branch** of the federal government. Article I specifically establishes that the legislative branch consists of a Senate and a House of Representatives that form a single Congress. Article I assigns specific powers to Congress, enabling it to:

- Make law
- Declare war
- Impeach elected or appointed officials
- Establish courts
- Levy taxes

Article I states Congress does *not* have the authority to:

- Create a law designed to affect a specific individual or group.
- Penalize an individual for an act that he or she committed prior to the passing of the law, providing the action was legal before the law was passed.
- Suspend the writ of habeas corpus, unless there is a rebellion or an invasion.

Second article:

The second article of the United States Constitution establishes the **executive branch** of the federal government. Article II specifically establishes that the executive branch consists of the President of the United States and his or her officers, whom the President appoints. Article II lists the powers granted to the President of the United States, including to:

- Enforce laws passed by Congress
- Appoint judges to the U.S. Supreme Court
- Appoint ambassadors
- Veto bills passed by Congress
- Command the army
- Negotiate and sign treaties

Article II limits the powers of the President. Congress may overturn a Presidential veto if two-thirds of the Senate and the House of Representatives vote to do so. The President may not enter into a treaty with another country without the consent of the Senate.

*Copyright © Mometrix Media. You have been licensed one copy of this document for personal use only. Any other reproduction or redistribution is strictly prohibited. All rights reserved.*

<u>Third article:</u>
The third article of the United States Constitution establishes the **judicial branch** of the federal government. Article III specifically establishes that the judicial branch consists of the United States Supreme Court and all of the lower courts created by Congress. Article III gives the courts the powers to:

- Hear and decide cases.
- Follow the system of jurisdictions to decide whether a federal court can hear a case or not.
- Order a trial by jury for any criminal case unrelated to an impeachment proceeding.
- Define the act of treason and the procedures to punish an individual or group for treason.

Article III states:

- Judges must be allowed to hold their positions for life, unless they choose to retire or they are impeached.
- Judges must receive compensation throughout their time in office without fear of that compensation being decreased.

**Bill of Rights**

The Bill of Rights includes the first ten amendments made to the Constitution. Each amendment grants specific rights to each citizen of the United States.

- The First Amendment to the Constitution protects an individual's rights to: Free speech; worship; petition the government; assembly; and freedom of the press.
- The Second Amendment to the Constitution protects an individual's right to: Bear arms (own a weapon).
- The Third Amendment to the Constitution protects the right of private individuals to refuse to house soldiers, unless there is a law explicitly saying that he or she must do so because the country is currently involved in a war.
- The Fourth Amendment to the Constitution protects an individual and his or her property from search and seizure, unless there is probable cause for an official to conduct a search.
- The Fifth Amendment to the Constitution grants an individual the rights to: Due process; refuse to testify to avoid self-incrimination; compensation for property taken for public use; avoid being tried twice for the same crime.
- The Sixth Amendment to the Constitution grants an individual the right to: Seek legal counsel; a speedy trial; a public trial; to confront the witnesses testifying against him or her in court.
- The Seventh Amendment to the Constitution grants an individual the right to a trial by jury in any civil case in which either party is seeking more than $20.
- The Eighth Amendment to the Constitution protects an individual from cruel and unusual punishment and prohibits the courts from imposing or requiring excessive fines or bail.

*Copyright © Mometrix Media. You have been licensed one copy of this document for personal use only. Any other reproduction or redistribution is strictly prohibited. All rights reserved.*

- The Ninth Amendment to the Constitution protects any right not specifically granted by the Constitution, providing that right is not held by the government alone or specifically prohibited through the use of a power granted to the government through the Constitution.
- The Tenth Amendment to the Constitution grants any powers that are not specifically granted to the federal government to each of the state governments.

## Fourteenth amendment to the United States Constitution

The Fourteenth Amendment to the United States Constitution primarily establishes that all U.S. citizens should have equal rights in the eyes of the law. Any person tried in a state court has the right to due process of law. Any law passed by a state government must protect every citizen within the state, and not just specific groups. State governments may not pass a law that eliminating or restricting the rights or protections of any U.S. citizen. The Fourteenth Amendment also defines which individuals are considered citizens. It establishes the system for determining the number of representatives for each state. The Fourteenth Amendment states a person convicted of treason while in a public office or after leaving office may not be elected to any other public office.

## Due process

The legal concept of due process means the person has the right to be treated fairly throughout the legal system. However, fair treatment is difficult to define. Due process means the representatives of local, state, and federal governments and courts must act reasonably and apply procedures consistently. The right of due process specifically applies to persons affected by a state or federal action, law, statute, or procedural rule. The person must be engaged in a legal action with a government representative or an organization that has a relationship with the government.

Types of due process:
The two main types of due process are procedural due process and substantive due process. **Procedural due process** refers to the specific actions a court or authority follows during the legal proceeding to ensure every person is treated in the same way as others were in the past. The person has a right to be given advance notice and to be heard. **Substantive due process** means the laws, rules, and regulations the government establishes must be fair and evenly applied. Statutes, rules, and regulations must be reasonable and well-defined. The lawyer monitors due process constantly to ensure the client's case is fairly handled. If you notice an infraction of due process, notify your principal immediately.

Substantive due process:
*Arbitrariness:* Arbitrariness means the content of a statute, rule, or regulation is written with no reasonable basis, in a subjective, illogical, or capricious way, or that

- 89 -

Copyright © Mometrix Media. You have been licensed one copy of this document for personal use only. Any other reproduction or redistribution is strictly prohibited. All rights reserved.

its purpose cannot be accomplished in a reasonable way. A statute, rule, or regulation is considered arbitrary when it is too broad or vague.

*Overbreadth:* Overbreadth is a type of arbitrariness in which a statute, rule, or regulation is too wide-ranging and extensive to accomplish its intended purpose in a reasonable way. The overbroad statute, rule, or regulation restricts more than its drafters originally intended because it is not specific enough.

*Vagueness:* Vagueness is a type of arbitrariness in which a law or rule is too indistinct and unclear to actually accomplish its intended purpose. A vague statute, rule, or regulation does distinguish what the intended purpose of the law or rule actually is.

## Right to notice

The right to notice is a fundamental concept associated with procedural due process. The right to notice means a representative of the government, such as a police officer or Court Clerk, informs the defendant as soon as possible when legal action is taken against him or her. The government representative can appear in-person or write to the defendant. The government representative explains:
- Why the legal action was initiated.
- The charges.
- The type of crime (felony, misdemeanor, or tort).
- The specific claims filed.

The government representative may be required to instruct the defendant how to proceed against that action.

## Right to be heard

The right to be heard is a fundamental concept associated with procedural due process, which states the person has the right to present his or her side of an issue at a hearing.

## Jurisdiction

Jurisdiction means the power of a court to render a decision in a specific area of law or the type of case a particular court is allowed to hear. For example, a bankruptcy court has no jurisdiction to hear a murder case.

Personal Jurisdiction:
Personal jurisdiction is also called *in personam* jurisdiction. If the court is asked to make a decision affecting parties in a legal action, then it must have power over them because they are residents or regularly do business there. For example, John and Joan marry and reside in Wisconsin. Joan moves to Arkansas and sues for

*Copyright © Mometrix Media. You have been licensed one copy of this document for personal use only. Any other reproduction or redistribution is strictly prohibited. All rights reserved.*

divorce. The Arkansas court grants Joan a divorce but cannot settle child custody, support payments, division of assets, or visitation because they affect John in Wisconsin and it has no personal jurisdiction over him.

## Subject Matter Jurisdiction:
Subject matter jurisdiction means the court has authority to resolve the thing in dispute. For example, Texas cannot grant a divorce unless one party has lived in the state 6 months, and in the same county 90 days. If the time requirement is unmet, a Texas judge cannot hear the case.

## Territorial Jurisdiction:
Territorial jurisdiction means a judge can hear any case filed in the catchment area that the court oversees.

## Jurisdiction In Rem:
The Latin phrase *in rem* literally means upon the thing. Jurisdiction *in rem* means the court exercises power over things but not persons. For example, Wisconsin has *in rem* jurisdiction over John and Joan's former family home because it is in Madison, but Arkansas has jurisdiction to end their marriage by divorce because Joan is a resident of Little Rock.

## Quasi In Rem Jurisdiction:
The Latin phrase *quasi in rem* literally means as if upon the thing. *Quasi in rem* jurisdiction means the court has the right to hear a case and enforce its judgment because one party owns real estate or property within its geographical catchment area. The party does not need to be present in the court for its decision to be binding.

## Exclusive Jurisdiction:
Exclusive jurisdiction means a court is the sole court granted the authority to hear a particular case.

## General Jurisdiction:
General jurisdiction means a court can hear any case that does not fall under the exclusive jurisdiction of another court. For example, a general-jurisdiction trial court hears any serious case and appeals from minor cases heard in lower courts.

## Limited Jurisdiction:
Limited jurisdiction indicates a tier system of courts. For example, a juvenile court is limited to hearing cases about minors, and a justice-of-the-peace is limited to deciding on minor criminal offenses and holding preliminary hearings for serious crimes that are then passed along to a superior court. Lower courts receive funding from local governments and higher courts are funded by the state.

*Copyright © Mometrix Media. You have been licensed one copy of this document for personal use only. Any other reproduction or redistribution is strictly prohibited. All rights reserved.*

Appellate Jurisdiction:

Appellate jurisdiction means the higher court can hear any case that has already been decided by a lower court if the decision is appealed. The higher court reviews the court documents; the appellant may not necessarily appear in person.

Concurrent Jurisdiction:

Concurrent jurisdiction means two or more courts share the authority to hear a particular case. It the opponents choose to take a legal action that falls under a concurrent jurisdiction, then they can file the action with either court.

Original Jurisdiction:

Original jurisdiction means a court is allowed to be the first court to hear a case.

Diversity of Citizenship Jurisdiction:

Diversity of citizenship jurisdiction means a court can hear a civil case involving citizens from different states or even different countries, provided it involves more than $75,000, without any interest or costs included. Diversity of citizenship cases are usually heard by the U.S. District Courts.

Discretionary Jurisdiction:

Discretionary jurisdiction means a court can decide whether it will hear a particular case or not. This is an important type of jurisdiction to note because most courts are required to hear *any* case that is filed, according to the procedures established by the court.

Federal Question Jurisdiction:

Federal question jurisdiction means a court can hear any case that is related to a violation of a federal law, a treaty, or a provision of the U.S. Constitution.

**Minimum Contacts**

Minimum contacts means the defendant must keep a residence or conduct business within the state in which a case is filed in order for a court within that state to make a decision that affects the defendant. In other words, a court can only issue a decision that affects a defendant if it has jurisdiction. The defendant has willingly entered the state or interacted with the state in some way.

**Long-arm statute**

A long-arm statute allows a court to order a defendant back to the state in which a case is filed to answer the claim or criminal charge.

Copyright © Mometrix Media. You have been licensed one copy of this document for personal use only. Any other reproduction or redistribution is strictly prohibited. All rights reserved.

## Venue

A venue is the specific location in which a defendant will be tried. The venue for a trial is usually in the area where the crime was committed, or the area in which the civil issue occurred, or the area in which the defendant lives, or the area in which the defendant owns property.

## Moving a case from state to federal court

There are four conditions that must be met in order for a defendant to remove a case from a state court to a federal court:

1. The federal court must have **original jurisdiction** for the type of case that is being removed from the state court. A case can only be removed if a federal court had the authority to hear the case before the state court actually hears it.
2. The state court from which the case is being removed must have **jurisdiction for the type of case** that is being removed from the state court. A case can only be removed from a state court that had the authority to hear the case.
3. The defendant must be a **resident of another state**, different from the state in which the state court is located.
4. If the case involves a diversity of citizenship, **all of the defendants and plaintiffs involved in the case must reside in separate states or countries** from the time that the case was filed with the state court.

## Writs

Writ of Ejectment:
A writ of ejectment is a legal document that orders a defendant to relinquish control of a particular piece of land or real estate to the plaintiff. A landowner can take civil action and request a court to eject an individual who is living on his or her property without his or her consent by requesting a writ of ejectment.

Writ of Certiorari:
A writ of certiorari is a legal document that orders a lower court to present any records that the lower court has for a particular case to a higher court. A defendant who appeals a court decision is required to request that a writ of certiorari.

Writ of Mandamus:
A writ of mandamus is a legal document that orders a court or a government officer to take a particular action or refrain from a particular action.

## Choice of law

Choice of law applies to a situation in which two or more states have laws affecting a particular case which contradict each other, so the court cannot rule based on the law alone. The court considers the laws from multiple states. For example, a vehicle

- 93 -

*Copyright © Mometrix Media. You have been licensed one copy of this document for personal use only. Any other reproduction or redistribution is strictly prohibited. All rights reserved.*

is stolen in Texas, used for a theft in Louisiana, and the contraband is driven to New York State, where the criminal attempts to sell it. Consequently, three states' laws cover the same crime. Choice of law questions are also called conflict of law questions. They most frequently occur because a case involves a civil violation that took place in two or more states or because a case is filed in a state other than the state in which the civil violation occurred.

Lex Fori:
The Latin phrase *lex fori* literally means law from the entrance. *Lex fori* is a method courts use to decide choice of law cases by using the laws from the state in which the case was originally filed.

Lex Loci Contractus:
The Latin phrase *lex loci contractus* literally means law from entering into the contract. *Lex loci contractus* means the court uses the laws of the state in which the contract was created to decide a choice of law question.

Lex Loci Solutionis:
The Latin phrase *lex loci solutionis* literally means law from the contract's solution. *Lex loci solutionis* means the court uses the laws of the state in which the provisions of the contract were supposed to be carried out to decide a choice of law question.

## Judgments made in another state

It is illegal for a state to refuse to enforce a judgment made in another state, unless the state that issued the judgment violated an individual's constitutional rights in issuing the judgment. This is because Article IV of the United States Constitution establishes that each state must recognize the validity of any public act, record, or judicial proceeding that is issued by another state. As a result, each state is required to enforce a judgment, even if it is made in another state, providing the ruling complies with constitutional provisions and the defendant's right to due process. An example would be enforcing a child support order issued in Texas when the delinquent parent moves to Alaska.

## Judgments made in another country

It is legal for a state to refuse to enforce a judgment made in another country if there is no reciprocal treaty. There is no blanket federal or international law that requires a state to recognize the validity of a judgment made in another country. However, if there is an extradition treaty, the defendant can be sent back to answer the charges. In practice, U.S. state and federal courts will typically recognize the validity of judgments made in other countries, even though they are not required to do so, *providing that judgment is reasonable*. This is because the state and federal courts of the United States observe the legal concept of **comity**, which establishes that the

Copyright © Mometrix Media. You have been licensed one copy of this document for personal use only. Any other reproduction or redistribution is strictly prohibited. All rights reserved.

courts will recognize the validity of judgments made in other countries as a courtesy to those countries.

## Advisory opinion

An advisory opinion is a comment in which a court identifies the judgment that it would issue if the facts related to a hypothetical case were actually presented to the court. A court may issue an advisory opinion if an individual asks the court to examine the facts of a case when that case is not actually being presented to the court. It is important to note that federal courts and certain state courts are prohibited from making advisory opinions.

## Collusive suit

A collusive suit is a type of lawsuit in which the plaintiffs and defendants agree to file the suit in order to determine the judgment that the court would issue in that particular case. Collusive suits are strictly prohibited in almost every jurisdiction.

## Validity of legal issues

Moot:
Moot describes a legal issue that is legally immaterial, irrelevant, or pointless and is therefore not actually a valid legal issue.

Ripe:
Ripe describes a legal issue that has fully developed or, in other words, is a valid legal issue.

## Immunity

Immunity refers to a legal protection in which an individual or organization cannot be tried for a civil and/or criminal offense.
Charitable Immunity:
Charitable immunity is available in some states for non-profit organizations, which cannot be tried for civil offenses.

Contractual Immunity:
Contractual immunity means an individual or organization cannot be tried for a civil offense because there is a contract between the defendant and the plaintiff protecting the defendant from legal action.

Parental Immunity:
Parental immunity is available in some states to protect parents from a civil offense suit related to the discipline of their children, unless the parent has committed

Copyright © Mometrix Media. You have been licensed one copy of this document for personal use only. Any other reproduction or redistribution is strictly prohibited. All rights reserved.

abuse or the child filing suit is emancipated (married at age 16 or self-supporting at age 16).

Sovereign Immunity:
Sovereign immunity means a government organization or a representative of a government organization performing his or her normal responsibilities cannot be tried for a civil or criminal offense.

## Litigation

Bar:
To bar means to prevent a lawsuit from being litigated for legal reasons. A bar is the specific reason that a lawsuit cannot be legally filed.

Res Judicata:
The Latin phrase *res judicata* literally means the judgment occurred. *Res judicata* is a type of bar in which a civil case cannot be filed because the case was already decided. If a defendant wins a civil case, the plaintiff in that case cannot file another suit based on the same facts as the case that was decided.

Statute of Limitations:
A statute of limitations is a type of bar in which a regulation sets the maximum amount of time that the complainant legally has to file a claim after a civil offense has occurred. It is important to note that a statute of limitations may be extended in certain situations. For example, there is no statute of limitations on murder, a federal crime.

## Court orders

Temporary Restraining Order:
A temporary restraining order (TRO) is a court order that prohibits an individual or group from taking a specific action until a hearing can be held. The applicant requesting a TRO must appear before a judge, prove that irreparable harm will be caused if the individual or the group is allowed to take the action, and prove that the individual or group will not be significantly harmed if they are prohibited from taking the action.
Temporary Injunction:
A temporary injunction is a court order that prohibits an individual or group from taking a specific action until a trial can be held. A temporary injunction will be issued if the need for a temporary restraining order is confirmed at a hearing.

Permanent Injunction:
A permanent injunction is a court order that prohibits an individual or group from taking a specific action at any time.

*Copyright © Mometrix Media. You have been licensed one copy of this document for personal use only. Any other reproduction or redistribution is strictly prohibited. All rights reserved.*

**Damages**

The four types of damages that a plaintiff can seek are:
1. Compensatory damages include any legal remedy in which an individual is compensated for the amount of money that he or she actually lost or the physical or mental harm that occurred as a result of a civil offense.
2. Liquidated damages include any legal remedy in which an individual receives the amount that a contract says the individual will receive from the other parties involved in the agreement if the contract is breached.
3. Nominal damages include any legal remedy in which an individual receives a small amount of money to make it clear that a civil offense was committed against the individual even though no actual financial harm was done.
4. Punitive damages include any legal remedy in which the court orders an individual who committed a civil offense to pay a certain amount of money to punish that individual for committing that offense.

Compensatory damages:
The two types of compensatory damages are:
1. General damages are compensatory damages that the court orders the defendant to give the plaintiff for the financial, physical or mental harm that any individual affected by that specific civil offense would sustain. General damages are reasonable estimates of costs.
2. Special damages are compensatory damages that that the court orders the defendant to pay the plaintiff for the exact amount of money that he or she actually lost due to the civil offense. Special damages may require receipts from the plaintiff for hotel rooms, taxi cabs, restaurant food, and replaced items. The plaintiff may have to prove loss of work and lack of insurance coverage.

**Alternative dispute resolution**

The three main types of alternative dispute resolution (ADR) are:
1. Arbitration, in which the parties involved in a dispute agree to allow an impartial arbitrator, who is not involved in the dispute, to hear all of the facts related to the dispute and makes a decision. It is important to note that the decision of an arbitrator is usually legally binding, but the decision may be appealed in court.
2. Mediation means the parties involved in a dispute agree to allow a mediator, who is not involved in the dispute, to hear all of the facts related to the dispute and offer his or her advice. Mediators only offer nonbinding opinions, so the parties involved in the dispute may subsequently take legal action if they choose to do so.
3. Court-annexed ADR means the court appoints an arbitrator or a mediator to hear the dispute in the hopes of achieving a compromise between the parties.

Copyright © Mometrix Media. You have been licensed one copy of this document for personal use only. Any other reproduction or redistribution is strictly prohibited. All rights reserved.

**Administrative agency powers**

Adjudication:
Adjudication is a process in which an administrative agency examines the facts related to a particular situation to determine if a violation of administrative law occurred. An administrative agency's adjudication process is often very similar to a civil trial, but the specific process that an agency uses can vary greatly from agency to agency. Note that some adjudication processes may involve procedures and practices that are completely different from the practices and procedures used in a standard civil trial.

Discretion:
Discretion refers to the ability of an administrative agency to create administrative law and decide issues related to administrative law. The administrative agency can decide which rules are necessary and how to adjudicate issues.

Rulemaking:
Rulemaking is the process in which an administrative agency creates administrative rules designed to address a particular issue and/or regulate a particular area of law.

## Business Organizations

**Business organizations**

Sole Proprietorship:
A sole proprietorship is a business organization in which a single owner operates the business in order to make a profit. A sole proprietorship is the easiest type of business to establish, but the business' liability rests solely with the individual who owns the business. The sole proprietor's personal assets can be seized to satisfy business claims.

Partnership:
A partnership is a business organization in which a group of individuals owns and operates the business together in order to make a profit. A partnership is no more difficult to establish than a sole proprietorship, but the business' liability is divided evenly amongst all of the partners involved.
*Limited Partnership* A limited partnership is a business organization in which a group of individuals owns and/or operates the business in order to make a profit, but the liability of each partner is restricted. A limited partnership is usually more difficult to establish than a partnership, but each partner is only liable for the amount that the partner has invested in the business.

Copyright © Mometrix Media. You have been licensed one copy of this document for personal use only. Any other reproduction or redistribution is strictly prohibited. All rights reserved.

Joint Stock Company:
A joint stock company is a business organization in which the owners contribute to a group operating fund to pay the business' operating expenses. A joint stock company is usually much easier to establish than a corporation, but all of the corporation's liability rests with the joint stock company's owners.

Corporation:
A corporation is a business organization that is considered to be a separate legal entity from the individuals who established or now own it. A corporation can exercise many rights usually granted to the citizens of a state because a corporation is considered to be a citizen of any state in which it does business and in which it was established. A corporation is much more difficult to establish than a sole proprietorship or a partnership, but each owner is only liable for the investment amount, and his/her personal assets usually cannot be seized.

Types of corporations include:
*Business Corporation:* A business corporation is a business entity established to make a profit.
*Nonprofit Corporation:* A nonprofit corporation is established to support a charity, church, or other enterprise for the public good.
*Public Corporation:* A public corporation is business entity created by the government to perform a certain task or a certain group of tasks.
*Publicly Held Corporation:* A publicly held corporation can sell shares to anyone interested in purchasing a portion of the organization.
*Private Corporation:* A private corporation is a business entity in which each share of the organization is owned by a specific group of people and there are no shares available to the general public.
*Professional Corporation:* A professional corporation is created by a group of licensed individuals, such as lawyers, doctors, or engineers who agreed to conduct business together.
*Chapter S Corporation:* A Chapter S corporation can require its shareholders to pay taxes on the corporation's income, so the corporation can avoid some of the corporate taxes that the corporation would otherwise be required to pay.
*Domestic Corporation:* A domestic corporation operates in the state in which the corporation was established.
*Foreign Corporation:* A foreign corporation operates in any state other than the state in which it was established.

Limited liability company:
A limited liability company (LLC) is a business organization that combines some of the advantages of a corporation with some of the advantages of a partnership. The two most important advantages of a limited liability company are that the owners of an LLC are typically liable for some, but not all of the business' activities, and the owners of the LLC typically can choose to file taxes as a sole proprietorship, a partnership, or a corporation. Limited liability companies are usually easier to

Copyright © Mometrix Media. You have been licensed one copy of this document for personal use only. Any other reproduction or redistribution is strictly prohibited. All rights reserved.

establish than corporations, but the specific process can vary greatly from state to state.

**Corporations**

Articles of Incorporation:
The articles of incorporation are a set of legal documents that a business must file in order for the business to be considered a corporation. Sometimes they are called the Corporate Charter. The articles of incorporation includes information related to the purpose of the corporation, the way that the organization is organized, and the individuals involved in the organization.

The information that a corporation is required to include in its articles of incorporation includes the:
- Corporation's name.
- Names and addresses of its initial Board of Directors.
- Location of its registered office.
- Length of time that the corporation is expected to exist.
- Purpose of the corporation.
- Decision to be a stock or a non-stock company.
- Decision to work for profit or not-for-profit.

In addition to the above information, most states also require the articles of incorporation to identify the type of corporation, the types of stock to be issued, the number of shares to be issued, and the rights that the corporation will grant to its stockholders.

Bylaws:
A bylaw is a rule that a corporation establishes to ensure it continues to function in an effective manner. Bylaws are recorded in writing and kept by the corporation itself.

Certificate of Incorporation:
A certificate of incorporation is a legal document issued by the Secretary of State in which the corporation was established. The certificate proves the business is actually a corporation. In order for a business to receive a certificate of incorporation, the business must meet all of the requirements established by the state in which the business is attempting to incorporate.

De jure Corporation:
The Latin phrase *de jure* can also be written as *de iure*. It literally means concerning the law or concerning the oath. A *de jure* corporation is a business that is considered to be a corporation in the eyes of the law. In order for a business to be considered a *de jure* corporation, the business must meet all of the requirements

*Copyright © Mometrix Media. You have been licensed one copy of this document for personal use only. Any other reproduction or redistribution is strictly prohibited. All rights reserved.*

established by the laws of the state in which the business is attempting to incorporate and the business must have a valid certificate of incorporation.

Promoter:
A promoter is an individual who designs a plan that explains the process that an organization should use to establish a corporation. A promoter identifies the specific steps that a business must take in order to incorporate and creates a description of these steps.

## Liability of a defective corporation

There are two situations in which the liability of a defective corporation may be limited:
1. The organization is considered to be a *de facto* corporation, which attempted to meet the legal requirements of the state in which the Board hoped to incorporate, but failed to meet those requirements. A *de facto* corporation may still receive some, but not all, of the benefits of an actual corporation, providing its officers made a reasonable effort to meet the legal requirements of the state.
2. Estoppel applies, meaning the owners of a defective corporation may not be held liable for the fact that a corporation is defective if the owners are sued by an individual or organization that did business with it, under the assumption that the organization was a valid corporation.

## Shareholder liability

The liability of a corporate shareholder is typically limited to the amount that the shareholder invested in the corporation. However, there are specific situations in which a court may ignore the protections typically granted to a corporation through a process known as "piercing the corporate veil." A court can ignore the limited liability granted to the shareholders if the corporation failed to:
- Hold stockholder meeting.
- Issue shares of stock.
- Invest enough in the corporation to keep it functional.

A court can also pierce the corporate veil if:
- A shareholder used the corporation to commit a wrongful act.
- The corporation actually consists of many smaller corporations.
- The activities and/or assets of the shareholders and the corporation itself are indistinguishable.

Note that a court will usually only hold a shareholder liable in these situations if the case involves a corporation with an extremely small number of shareholders or if the shareholder committed a wrongful act.

Copyright © Mometrix Media. You have been licensed one copy of this document for personal use only. Any other reproduction or redistribution is strictly prohibited. All rights reserved.

## Corporate finances

*Capital Structure:* Capital structure refers to the state of a corporation's finances, specifically its debt and equity.

*Dividends:* A dividend is a payment that a corporation issues to shareholders to distribute some of its profits as money or a certain amount of stock that is paid per share.

*Par Value:* Par value is the amount of money that an individual pays a corporation to obtain a security when it first begins selling that particular type of security. It is important to note that the par value of a security is the minimum amount for which a security can be sold.

*Security:* A security is anything that legally indicates that an individual owns a share of a corporation or that a corporation has an obligation to repay a debt to another individual or organization.

*Stock certificate:* A stock certificate is a legal document that indicates that an individual owns a share of stock.

## Stocks

*Common stock:* Common stock grants a shareholder the right to vote on corporate matters, but he/she only receives dividends if the corporation still has funds remaining after all of the preferred shareholders have received dividends.

*Convertible stock:* Convertible stock is also known as exchangeable stock. Convertible stock allows a shareholder to change his or her shares into another type of stock. Note that a shareholder can only convert his or her stock to a type of stock that has fewer rights than the stock the individual holds currently.

*Preferred stock:* Preferred stock means the shareholder receives dividends before any dividends are paid to common stock shareholders. However, preferred stock does not necessarily grant voting rights to shareholders.

The most common types of preferred stock a corporation may issue are:

- Cumulative preferred stock, for which the shareholder receives a dividend for the year in which the corporation issued the payment and a dividend for each year prior to that year in which the corporation did not pay a dividend to the shareholder
- Non-cumulative preferred stock, for which the shareholder receives a dividend payment for any year in which the corporation pays a dividend
- Participating preferred stock means the shareholder receives the dividend established by the corporation for preferred stock owners and the dividend to which a common stock shareholder is entitled
- Nonparticipating preferred stock means the shareholder only receives the dividend established by the corporation.

*Redeemable stock:* Redeemable stock means the corporation can buy it back from its shareholders at a price established by the corporation at the time the stock was issued.

Copyright © Mometrix Media. You have been licensed one copy of this document for personal use only. Any other reproduction or redistribution is strictly prohibited. All rights reserved.

*Preemptive Rights:* A pre-emptive right is a benefit granted to privileged individuals who can purchase common stock before the corporation actually makes that stock available on the open market.

*Stock Options:* A stock option is a benefit in which an individual receives stock automatically or can purchase stock at a discount or a set rate.

*Stock Subscription:* A stock subscription means an individual agrees to purchase some of the shares that a corporation has not actually issued yet.

*Stock Rights:* A stock right is a legal document that indicates an individual has the right to exercise a short-term stock option.

*Stock Warrants:* A stock warrant is a legal document that indicates an individual has the right to exercise a long-term stock option.

## Securities

*Bond:* A bond is a type of security (debt) a corporation is obligated to repay that is secured by collateral.

*Debenture:* A debenture is a type of security (debt) a corporation is obligated to repay, but that debt is not secured by any collateral.

*Notes:* A note, also called a promissory note, is a type of security in which a corporation agrees to repay a loan obtained from a bank.

## Leverage

Leverage, which is also called trading on equity, means a business is able to earn a larger profit from borrowing money than the business would have to pay in interest for borrowing that money.

## Trust Indenture

A trust indenture is a legal document that indicates that a financial institution has issued bonds or debentures on behalf of a corporation.

## Shareholder voting

The two types of shareholder voting are:
1. Cumulative voting, used when a corporation's shareholders elects the Board of Directors.  The number of shares the shareholder owns is multiplied by the number of seats available on the Board of Directors to determine the total number of votes that the shareholder can cast.  Cumulative voting is required in certain states, but it is not required in every state.
2. Straight voting means each shareholder will receive one vote for each share he/she owns.  Straight voting is the most common type of shareholder voting.

*Copyright © Mometrix Media. You have been licensed one copy of this document for personal use only. Any other reproduction or redistribution is strictly prohibited. All rights reserved.*

Note that shareholders can assign their voting rights to another individual or another organization through a written document known as a **proxy**, regardless of the type of voting that is used.

### Revised Model Business Corporation Act

The Revised Model Business Corporation Act (RMBCA) is a set of regulations designed by the American Bar Association to address legal issues related to corporations. RMBCA describes the:

- Characteristics that make a business a corporation.
- Duties and responsibilities of a corporation.
- Rights that can and cannot be granted to shareholders.
- Rights and responsibilities of directors.

Most states have adopted the regulations established by the Revised Model Business Corporation Act. As a result, corporations are required to adhere to the regulations established by the RMBCA in those states. However, it is important to note that the regulations established by the Revised Model Business Corporation Act are only suggested regulations, so a corporation may not be required to adhere to the RMBCA in every state.

### Mergers and acquisitions

Mergers and acquisitions are similar in many ways. Both refer to a type of structural change in which two corporations join together, so their operations are controlled by a single corporation. However, they are two separate processes. A **merger** creates a single corporation because the interests of both corporations will be better served through the merger. After the merger, one of the corporations is legally dissolved. Its assets and operations are merged into the surviving corporation. An **acquisition** occurs when Corporation A purchases enough stock in Corporation B to exercise control over Corporation B. After the acquisition, both corporations still exist. Corporation A decides all future actions, whether Corporation B agreed to the purchase or not.

### EEOC

The Equal Opportunity Employment Commission (EEOC) was formed by Title VII of the *Civil Rights Act* to protect vulnerable groups from unlawful discrimination. The EEOC is a federal agency that encourages minorities to work in jobs previously closed to them. EEOC trains employers to avoid practices and policies that could cause unlawful discrimination and enforces the laws included in the Civil Rights Act (CRA) and the Age Discrimination in Employment Act (ADEA). EEOC is authorized to negotiate settlements with employers who engaged in discrimination. If the EEOC cannot come to an agreement with an employer, the EEOC files suit against

Copyright © Mometrix Media. You have been licensed one copy of this document for personal use only. Any other reproduction or redistribution is strictly prohibited. All rights reserved.

the employer on behalf of the victim of the discrimination to enforce the anti-discrimination law.

## Occupational Safety and Health Act

The Occupational Safety and Health Act (OSHA) of 1970 established the U.S. Department of Labor's Occupational Safety & Health Administration. OSHA requires employers to keep the work area safe and free of hazards that could cause injury, death, or reproductive impairment. The employer appoints a Safety Officer to check http://www.osha.gov regularly for important updates that must be adopted as standards of practice. The Safety Officer trains employees in safe practice at the employer's expense. The employer must supply every employee with free personal protective equipment (PPE) appropriate to the work conditions. The Safety Officer ensures the PPE is kept clean and in good repair at no cost to the employee. OSHA defines how the worker can behave; for example, it restricts eating, smoking and applying make-up in contaminated areas. The employer must log and report every incident when an injury occurs or a physical hazard is released into the workplace in an uncontrolled way because a container breaks or leaks, or if storage or testing equipment malfunctions.

## National Labor Relations Act

The National Labor Relations Act (NLRA) is also known as the Wagner Act. NLRA grants certain rights to unionized workers or employees who want to unionize. NLRA states employees have the right to form a union, join a union, and take part in union activities. The NLRA protects the right to collective bargaining with the employer, regardless of whether the employees are union members or not. The regulations established by the NLRA do not apply to workers covered by the Railway Labor Act, farm workers, independent contractors, the immediate family of an employer, managers, supervisors, or to any other individual with the authority to make labor decisions on behalf of an employer.

## Civil Litigation

### Party

A party is an individual or a group is identified as the plaintiff or defendant in a lawsuit.

Indispensible Party:
An indispensible party is an individual or a group who must appear as the plaintiff or defendant and participate in a court proceeding, so the judge can hear a lawsuit and render a fair decision. The appearance is essential to the proceeding.

Copyright © Mometrix Media. You have been licensed one copy of this document for personal use only. Any other reproduction or redistribution is strictly prohibited. All rights reserved.

<u>Necessary Party:</u>
A necessary party is an individual or a group that should be allowed to appear as a defendant or plaintiff and participate in a court proceeding, but the participation is only optional and not required. The judge could still hear the lawsuit and render a fair decision in the necessary party's absence.

## Impleader

An impleader is a legal procedure in which a defendant is allowed to bring another defendant into the suit on the grounds that he/she was actually responsible for the civil offense of which the defendant is accused. For example, a Toyota driver is accused of damaging a Cadillac, but the accident only occurred because the Toyota spun out of control when it was rear-ended by a Fiat. The Toyota driver brings the Fiat driver into the suit as the originator of the accident. A defendant who initiates an impleader procedure is still considered to be the defendant of the lawsuit in which he or she is identified. However, the defendant is also considered to be a third-party plaintiff who is bringing a third-party claim against the individual accused of initiating the civil offense. The procedures for impleader are established by Rule 14 of the Federal Rules of Civil Procedure.

## Interpleader

An interpleader is a legal procedure that allows a plaintiff to bring two defendants into a lawsuit on the grounds that both those individuals may be able to make a claim for the same funds or benefit. The plaintiff who initiates an interpleader procedure is considered to be a stakeholder in the suit. The defendants are considered to be claimants who are required to participate in the suit so the court may determine which individual is entitled to the money or benefit. For example, a man with a life insurance policy dies, leaving a single surviving son. However, the life insurance policy identifies the policyholder's former spouse as the beneficiary of the policy. There are actually two individuals who may be able to claim the benefits — the ex-wife and son. In this situation, the life insurance company files an interpleader to make the son and former spouse both appear before the court. The procedures for interpleader are established by Rule 22 of the Federal Rules of Civil Procedure and federal statutes established in 28 U.S.C. §1335.

## Intervention

Intervention is a legal procedure that allows an individual to join a lawsuit even though he/she was not originally identified as a defendant or a plaintiff. There are situations in which a court *may* allow an individual to join a lawsuit and situations in which a court *must* allow it because that individual would be affected by the lawsuit. For example, a large business rents out office space in one of its buildings. The business is sued for failing to repay a loan intended to pay its general expenses. A renter may be able to intervene in the lawsuit if the suit identifies the building

*Copyright © Mometrix Media. You have been licensed one copy of this document for personal use only. Any other reproduction or redistribution is strictly prohibited. All rights reserved.*

where he or she rents office space as property that could be used to repay the loan. The procedures for intervention are established by Rule 24 of the Federal Rules of Civil Procedure and a number of federal statutes.

## Class action

A **class action**, also known as a representative action, is a lawsuit in which a civil offense has affected so many people that it is not realistically possible for the court to allow all of them to participate in the lawsuit. As a result, the plaintiff in the class action files suit on behalf of all of the people who have been affected by the offense of which the defendant has been accused. However, in order for an individual to file a class action, he/she must meet three requirements. Firstly, it must be unrealistic or impossible for the court to hear all of the individuals affected by the offense. Secondly, the individuals affected by the offense must have been affected in a similar way, so that the representatives of those individuals can make similar legal claims. Finally, the representatives of the affected individuals must be able to represent the entire group fairly and not just the interests of a single individual.

## Consolidation

Consolidation is a legal procedure that allows a court to combine two or more lawsuits into a single suit, providing those lawsuits are related to a similar claim. If the court is asked to hear two or more cases related to the same situation or civil offense, then it can consolidate those cases into a single case and hear them all at once. For example, five different individuals file five separate lawsuits against the same corporation, accusing it of engaging in fraudulent business practices. In this situation, the court decides to consolidate the five lawsuits into a single suit against the corporation with all five individuals acting as the plaintiff in the suit, so the court can save time and money.

## Motion

A motion is a legal action where an individual or a group asks a court to issue a court order prohibiting or requiring another party to take a specific action in relation to a specific case, or asks a court to make a decision related to a specific aspect of a case. A motion may be filed on many different grounds, but an individual must have a specific legal reason to petition the court for relief in order to file a motion.

## Pleading

A pleading is a legal document that is filed with a court in writing by the plaintiff and defendant or prosecutor and accused making allegations and counterallegations.

*Copyright © Mometrix Media. You have been licensed one copy of this document for personal use only. Any other reproduction or redistribution is strictly prohibited. All rights reserved.*

<u>Types of pleading:</u>
Courts have used code pleading and notice pleading since 1948. Code pleading means the official documents that a defendant or a plaintiff files with the court for a particular case must identify and describe all of the facts related to the case. Notice pleading means the official documents that a defendant or a plaintiff files with the court for a particular case are *only* required to notify the court and the other parties involved in the case of the legal actions or defenses involved in the case.

Common law pleading is an obsolete type that ended in the 19th century, but the paralegal will see it when researching precedents. The plaintiff filed a *Form of Action* with the court to issue a writ summoning the defendant. It had to be filed in a very specific way, with exact wording. If the wording was incorrect or there was no writ that covered the exact situation, then the judge threw out the case. Plaintiff and defendant could only take one position.

<u>Pleadings an individual may file:</u>
The three pleadings that an individual may file according to the Federal Rules of Civil Procedure are answers, complaints, and replies. An answer is a pleading in which a defendant responds to a complaint. A defendant is typically required to answer a complaint within 20 days from the date that the defendant is served with a summons related to that complaint, but may extend his or her time to answer to 60 days if he or she signs and sends back a form known as a waiver of service. A complaint is a pleading in which a plaintiff files a claim against a defendant. It is important to note that a complaint is required to bring a civil case before a federal court. A reply is a pleading in which a plaintiff responds to a defendant's counterclaim.

*Preparing a complaint:* The information contained in a complaint can vary from jurisdiction to jurisdiction. However, every complaint should start with the heading "Complaint" near the top of the pleading. An *ad damnum* clause asks the court to render a decision on the legal matter presented in the complaint. Include a statement that identifies the court, the defendant, and the plaintiff. Include a brief description of the claim, state the legal grounds on which the claim is based, and list the damages or relief that the plaintiff is seeking. Add a date and signature from the lawyer(s) representing the plaintiff.

*Answering a complaint:* There are four responses that a defendant is allowed to provide when answering a complaint:
1. To confirm that he or she actually committed *all* of the civil offenses identified in the complaint.
2. To confirm that he or she committed *some* of the offenses identified in the complaint, but not all of them. A court may issue a judgment for the offenses that the defendant admits and schedule a proceeding to hear information related to the other offenses he/she denies.

*Copyright © Mometrix Media. You have been licensed one copy of this document for personal use only. Any other reproduction or redistribution is strictly prohibited. All rights reserved.*

3. To deny all of the allegations.
4. To state that he or she does not have enough information to confirm or deny the offenses identified in the complaint.

## Counterclaims

The two types of counterclaims that a defendant may file are compulsory counterclaims and permissive counterclaims. Compulsory counterclaims mean the defendant files a claim against the plaintiff that is related to the same situation described in the lawsuit. The defendant must file his or her claim during the legal process associated with the lawsuit or lose the right to file the claim after the lawsuit has been decided. Permissive counterclaims, mean the defendant files a claim against the plaintiff for a completely separate situation than that associated with the lawsuit. A permissive claim may be filed at any time.

## Discovery meetings

The parties involved in a lawsuit are required to provide information to each other within 10 days of the discovery meeting. The specific information that a party is required to disclose can vary greatly from case to case. However, each party is required to provide the other party with the address, full name, and phone number of anyone with information relevant to the case. Each party must describe the type of information and any documents that are relevant to the case. The defendant must notify the plaintiff of any liability insurance he/she holds. The plaintiff must describe the damages he/she is seeking and the method used to determine those damages.

## Interrogatory

An interrogatory is a legal document that lists a series of questions the recipient is required to answer. Interrogatories are written by each of the parties involved in a dispute, so that each party can ask the other party for specific information that may be related to the case.

## Deposition

A deposition is a legal document or a recording that records a witness' testimony in the witness' own words, so that the testimony may be used in court. Depositions may be based on a written list of questions or on a series of verbal questions that the witness is asked to answer and each response is then recorded, videotaped, or written down.

Copyright © Mometrix Media. You have been licensed one copy of this document for personal use only. Any other reproduction or redistribution is strictly prohibited. All rights reserved.

## Subpoena

A subpoena is a legal document that requires an individual to testify before the court. Subpoenas may be issued by a Court Clerk or an attorney acting as an officer of the court.

Subpoena Duces Tecum:
A **subpoena duces tecum** is a legal document that requires an individual to bring any items that may be related to the case when he or she testifies before the court.

## Types of requests

*Request to Admit:* A request to admit, also known as a request for admissions, is a legal document in which a party lists a series of statements that the party is asking the other party to confirm, deny, or identify a reason for which the party can neither confirm nor deny the statement.
*Request for Medical Examination:* A request for mental examination is a legal document that a party files with the court asking for a court order requiring an individual to submit to an evaluation by a psychiatrist or psychologist because that individual's mental state is directly related to the dispute.
*Request for Physical Examination:* A request for physical examination is a legal document that a party files with the court asking for a court order requiring an individual to submit to an examination by an independent doctor because the individual's physical state is directly related to the dispute. It specifies a general practitioner or specialist.
*Request for Production:* A request for production is a legal document that requests a party to "produce" any information that may be related to the case.

## Immunity covering documents

When an attorney prepares a document, it might have absolute immunity or qualified immunity. Absolute immunity means a party is not required to disclose a particular document because it describes the attorney's legal strategy or a legal interpretation directly related to that strategy. Qualified immunity means a party is not required to disclose a particular document unless the opponent can prove the document provides information necessary to prove its case and is the only document that will provide that information. Qualified immunity is typically granted to a document that an attorney prepares specifically to aid his or her client in court.

## Case dismissal

The two ways that a case can be dismissed are with prejudice and without prejudice. A case dismissed with prejudice is terminated so that the claim associated with that case cannot be filed again under any circumstances. Cases dismissed with prejudice

*Copyright © Mometrix Media. You have been licensed one copy of this document for personal use only. Any other reproduction or redistribution is strictly prohibited. All rights reserved.*

are based on legal grounds considered to be ridiculous or unreasonable, filed simply to annoy or harass the defendant or another group, or the plaintiff has requested to dismiss the case on more than one occasion. A case dismissed without prejudice is terminated, but the claim associated with that case can be filed again. A case will typically be dismissed without prejudice if there was a judicial error, or at the request of the plaintiff, or if the case was filed on valid legal grounds but the plaintiff did not have enough information to actually prove that a civil offense occurred.

## Types of judgment

*Default Judgment:* A default judgment is a court decision in which a court rules against the defendant he/she failed to answer a complaint or failed to take another action required to defend in court.

*Partial Summary Judgment:* A partial summary judgment is a court decision in which a court rules on *some, but not all* of the claims presented in a particular case before it is officially tried. Any claims not decided as part of the partial summary judgment are heard when the case is tried.

*Summary Judgment:* A summary judgment is a court decision in which a court rules on *all* of the claims presented in a particular case before it is officially tried.

*General Verdict:* A general verdict is a court decision in which a judge or a jury states that the court is ruling in favor of the defendant or that the court is ruling in favor of the plaintiff.

*Hung Jury:* A hung jury means the jury cannot issue a verdict because a unanimous decision is required and they are unable to come to a consensus (complete agreement) regarding how the case should be decided.

*Special Verdict:* A special verdict is a court decision in which a jury describes the situation that occurred in the case as they understand it, and ask the judge to use his or her knowledge of the law to issue a decision based on those facts.

## Motion for a new trial

There are five situations in which a court may grant a party's motion for a new trial:
1. A party received new evidence unobtainable during the trial.
2. The verdict issued by the court was affected by an attorney, a juror, a party, or a witness who acted inappropriately.
3. The court made a judicial error.
4. Damages established by a verdict are unreasonably low or unreasonably high, considering the nature of the offense and/or the legal limits that have been established for damages related to that type of offense.
5. It is apparent that a verdict was issued in spite of the evidence or issued based on faulty evidence.

Copyright © Mometrix Media. You have been licensed one copy of this document for personal use only. Any other reproduction or redistribution is strictly prohibited. All rights reserved.

# Contracts

## Types of contracts

A contract is a binding promise to do something legal, which can be enforced in a court of law. The two types of contracts that an individual or organization may enter into are:

1. An expressed contract, where two or more individuals or organizations agree to perform a certain task or accept responsibilities established in a written document or verbal conversation.
2. An implied contract, where two or more individuals or organizations perform an action that makes it clear they accept certain tasks or responsibilities. For example, if a homeowner allows a carpenter to fix a door, they enter into an implied contract where the homeowner agrees to pay the carpenter for fixing the door, even though it is not actually stated or in writing.

## Contract forms

*Bilateral Contract:* A bilateral contract is the most common form of contract. Both parties agree to perform specific tasks or make mutually agreed-upon payments. For example a house purchase is a bilateral contract in which the seller agrees to give the buyer the title to the property in exchange for the sale price.

*Quasi-contract:* A quasi-contract is a legal situation in which a contract is said to exist because an individual or an organization received a significant benefit as a result of the actions taken by another party, even though there is no official agreement.

*Unilateral Contract:* A unilateral contract is less common than a bilateral contract. An example of a unilateral contract is a cat owner who tapes a reward poster to a telephone pole. The neighbor is not obliged to look for the cat or even to report seeing the cat if he does. However, if the neighbor returns the cat to its owner, then the owner must pay the reward money. The unilateral contract is a one-sided promise.

*Unenforceable Contract:* An unenforceable contract is valid but the court will not compel the parties perform it. For example, in jurisdictions where prostitution is legal, the court will not compel a prostitute to perform the sex act or the customer to pay when they have a dispute.

*Voidable Contract:* A voidable contract means one party can invalidate the contract if he/she chooses to do so. A voidable contract is only invalid if the party who holds the right to void exercises it.

*Void Contract:* A void contract or a void agreement means there never was a legal contract. Void contracts typically require an individual to perform a task that is illegal or completely impossible for anyone to perform.

Copyright © Mometrix Media. You have been licensed one copy of this document for personal use only. Any other reproduction or redistribution is strictly prohibited. All rights reserved.

## Enforcing a contract

There are three conditions that a contract must meet in order for the contract to be enforced:
1. All of the parties involved in the contract must demonstrate that they willingly intend to comply with its terms. One party cannot be coerced into signing by the other party. If a signor never intended to complete the contract, then it was never valid.
2. There cannot be any legal defense a party could use to dispute the terms of the contract.
3. The contract must offer some sort of exchange between the parties involved in it. For example, a contract may describe pay-for-service or exchange of title for money.

## Misrepresentation and fraud

Misrepresentation and fraud are very similar legal concepts. The major difference is the belief of the perpetrator. Misrepresentation means a contract was entered into when one party believed the information to be true when the information was actually false. Fraud occurs when an agreement was based on information one party knew to be false. The judgment hinges on whether the party who gave the incorrect information knowingly intended to provide false information. The bad intent to deceive that must be present in order for a statement to be considered fraud is known as **scienter**.

## Contract offers

The information that an individual or an organization should include in a contract offer can vary from offer to offer. However, every offer should contain these basics:
- Identify the individual or organization to whom the offer is being extended.
- Identify the property with a detailed description (e.g., address, lot number, serial number or valuation).
- Describe the terms and conditions of the offer as specifically as possible.
- Indicate the price that the buyer will pay and the seller will accept, or the specific service the parties will render if the contract is accepted.
- Identify a time frame in which the first party who is making the offer will issue payment or render the service to the second party.
- List any penalties that will occur if the contract is breached.
- Specify which laws govern the contract (which state, municipality, or federal jurisdiction), in case a dispute does arise later.

*Copyright © Mometrix Media. You have been licensed one copy of this document for personal use only. Any other reproduction or redistribution is strictly prohibited. All rights reserved.*

<u>Termination:</u>
There are four situations in which a contract offer will be terminated:
1. The contract is not accepted within the time frame established by the offer, or within a reasonable length of time after it is made, if no specific time limit is indicated.
2. The recipient of an offer refuses it outright.
3. The party who made the offer retracts it or informs the recipient that the offer is no longer available.
4. The offer is no longer valid under law because one party is dead, insane, or declared incompetent.

## Valid contracts

These conditions must be met in order for an accepted offer to become a valid contract:
1. The recipient of the offer must be the individual or organization to which the offer was originally made. If an offer is made to the general public, the offer may be accepted by any individual or organization.
2. The recipient must accept the terms of the offer as stated, *unless* the offer is related to the sale of a product. If a sale is involved, then a sign-back or counteroffer can be made, negotiating the terms of the agreement. The offer will not actually become a contract until the counteroffer is accepted by the first party who made the initial offer.
3. The recipient must notify the first party who issued the offer that the offer has been accepted while it is still valid.

<u>Challenging the validity of a contract:</u>
There are five legal defenses used to challenge the validity of a contract:
1. A mistake was made when the contract was written or transmitted.
2. One of the parties involved was incapable of entering into the contract because he/she was a minor, or was impaired by alcohol or drugs, or was incompetent to make his or her own decisions. Incompetence can be temporary, due to mental illness, or permanent, due to genetic disorder or brain injury.
3. One of the parties involved was coerced (forced) to agree to the contract by threats or physical force, pressurized to sign, or under undue influence.
4. The terms of the contract are offensive and unreasonable.
5. The terms of the contract actually violate a law or may cause an individual to violate a law.

Copyright © Mometrix Media. You have been licensed one copy of this document for personal use only. Any other reproduction or redistribution is strictly prohibited. All rights reserved.

## Mistakes to avoid

The four types of mistakes that any party entering into a contract must avoid are:
1. Unilateral mistake, in which one of the parties involved in the contract misunderstands its terms or a fact related to the contract.
2. Mutual mistake, which both parties misunderstand the terms or a fact related to the contract.
3. Value mistake, in which both parties believe that the products or services exchanged in the contract are worth less than they actually are.
4. Transmission mistake, in which one of the parties misunderstands the terms of the contract or misinterprets a response related to the contract because the information was distorted during the delivery process.

## Statute of Frauds

A state's Statute of Frauds identifies the types of agreements that must be stated in writing and signed by the parties involved. The agreements covered vary from state to state. However, most states cover agreements in which:
- One party will be responsible for repaying the debt of another.
- One party will purchase a piece of real estate or will use a piece of real estate for a specific purpose.
- A specific product will be sold for more than $499, unless that product was specifically ordered made for the individual or organization by request.

The Statute of Frauds applies to:
- Any agreement related to a marriage.
- Arrangements to pay the debts of an estate.
- Cases where the agreement cannot be carried out within one year from the signature date.

## Parties in a contract

*Delegate:* A delegate is an individual who performs a specific service or task in the stead of the party who agreed to do it by contract. A delegate represents the signatory to the contract.

*Promisor:* A promisor makes a promise to a promisee.

*Promisee:* A promisee is the party to whom something is promised.

*Third-party Beneficiary:* A third-party beneficiary is not a signatory to a contract, but has the right to enforce the contract or is entitled to a share of the benefits. For example, grandparents pay a down payment on a house for their grandson. The seller subsequently refuses to sell the house. The grandson can sue the seller as a third-party beneficiary who expected to benefit from the sale, although he did not contribute to the down payment or sign the contract.

*Copyright © Mometrix Media. You have been licensed one copy of this document for personal use only. Any other reproduction or redistribution is strictly prohibited. All rights reserved.*

## Discharging contract obligations

There are four situations in which an individual's contract obligations may be discharged:
1.  The first party performed his or her obligations or was prepared to perform them, but was unable to do so because the second party refused to allow performance.
2.  The party is no longer able to perform those tasks because it is now physically impossible for anyone to do so, illegal to do so, or it is no longer reasonable to expect a person to do so because a major unexpected change has occurred.
3.  Both parties agree to rescind the contract or establish a new contract that will take the place of the old contract.
4.  Both parties agree to modify the obligations established by the contract.

## Excusing a contract condition

There are four situations in which a condition identified by a contract may be excused:
1.  A party to the contract does not receive the specific or almost identical benefit promised in the contract.
2.  One party to the contract deliberately prevented the other party from performing his/her obligations related to that condition.
3.  One party to the contract refuses to perform his/her obligations.
4.  The party who benefits from a condition chooses to waive it.

## Breach of contract

A minor breach of contract occurs when a very similar product is substituted for the promised product and does not meet *all* conditions agreed upon.  The non-breaching party may collect some damages but not an order for performance, for example:  A contract calls for mechanic to install a *green* carburetor in the buyer's car.  The mechanic installs a *brass* carburetor from the same manufacturer of equal value and function.  No damages are awarded because the carburetor is usually hidden under the hood. The buyer did not experience a true loss just because the color was different.

A material breach means the buyer did not get products or services of equal value to those promised.  For example, the mechanic installed a cheap, inferior carburetor that would not last as long as the one paid for.  The judge issues a performance order so the mechanic installs exactly what was ordered.  If the buyer also lost work time due to the dispute, the judge may award damages.

*Copyright © Mometrix Media. You have been licensed one copy of this document for personal use only. Any other reproduction or redistribution is strictly prohibited. All rights reserved.*

# Practice Test

## *Practice Questions*

*The following sentences are either verbose or contain a grammar error. No sentence contains more than one error. Choose option A if the sentence is verbose or uses incorrect grammar or option B if the sentence contains neither type of error.*

1. We must examine all of the facts that have been presented before us first before we can come to a conclusion which is tenable.
   a.
   b.

2. Neither the defendant nor his attorney were able to come to an agreement as to how to proceed.
   a.
   b.

*Identify the correct word and circle it.*

3. Joanne could see her dog (laying) (lying) in front of the fireplace.

*The following sentence may contain an error in grammar, word usage, or punctuation, or it may be correct. Choose the underlined section that must be corrected or select option "E" if there is no error.*

4. One precedent, <u>not discussed in class,</u> for holding a hospital <u>liable</u> for the
                  a                                b
   malpractice of a physician <u>who is affiliated</u> with the hospital is the theory of
                                    c
   <u>Respondeat Superior.</u> <u>(No error)</u>
             d              e
   a.
   b.
   c.
   d.
   e.

5. True or false. You have interviewed two different witnesses and each one has given a different version of an incident. You can reasonably make the assumption then that one of them is not telling the truth.

*Copyright © Mometrix Media. You have been licensed one copy of this document for personal use only. Any other reproduction or redistribution is strictly prohibited. All rights reserved.*

6. An objective of the Unauthorized Practice of Law (UPL) statute is to
   a. Allow paralegals to accept cases.
   b. Comply with a client's request for information.
   c. Prevent paralegals from practicing law.
   d. All of the above
   e. None of the above

7. True or false. It is not an infraction of the UPL for a paralegal to give legal advice to a client, as long as the client does not pay for the advice.

8. It is ethical for a legal assistant to
   a. Review a client's complaint.
   b. Help a client execute his will.
   c. Explain to a client what his appeal procedures entail.
   d. Two of the above
   e. All of the above

9. A Chinese Wall can best be defined as
   a. A conceptual barrier that prohibits the flow of information.
   b. A conflict of interest directive.
   c. A firewall which prevents adverse parties from contact with a case.
   d. None of the above
   e. All of the above

10. An attorney must keep client funds in a separate account from an operating funds account because of which of the following?
   a. Treasury Department Circular No. 230
   b. IRS regulations
   c. Ethics rules
   d. Two of the above
   e. All of the above

11. True or false. It is customary for a paralegal to exercise his or her opinion in matters relating to procedure.

12. True or false. Juan, a legal assistant with five years of experience, overhears some law clerks in the lunch room discussing rumors about a senior partner. It is his duty to report them to his supervising attorney as soon as possible.

13. Precinct is to captain as _____ is to _____.
   a. policeman : beat
   b. president : congress
   c. hospital : surgeon
   d. manager : director

*Copyright © Mometrix Media. You have been licensed one copy of this document for personal use only. Any other reproduction or redistribution is strictly prohibited. All rights reserved.*

14. Veronica is a paralegal for attorney Joel Colby. For years, Joel's practice has been to send her copies of all his email correspondence with clients. For several months now, Veronica finds that Joel's clients keep emailing her because he is not responding to them. Which of the following is the best course of action for Veronica?
   a. Go to the senior partner and ask him what to do about Joel.
   b. Ask the senior partner if she can be transferred to another supervising attorney.
   c. Go online and see what kind of paralegal openings there are in other firms.
   d. Take Joel to lunch and ask what she can do to help him keep up with his email.

15. Six is to nine as ____ is to ____.
   a. 12 : 8
   b. 14 : 21
   c. 1 : 3
   d. 12 : 20

16. Some shih tzus are grey. Some grey dogs are good at agility. Some dogs good at agility are not shih tzus. Based on these propositions, which of the following could be true?
   a. No grey dogs are good at agility.
   b. No dogs good at agility are grey.
   c. Some shih tzus are good at agility
   d. All grey dogs are shih tzus.
   e. All shih tzus are good at agility.

17. Leonid has been given several cartons of paper involving a bankruptcy case. The attorney tells him everything has to be ready by the end of the week because that is when the claim must be filed. Leonid does not see how it can all be done because he has other deadlines approaching. Which of the following is the best course of action for Leonid?
   a. Tell the attorney that there is no way he can have everything ready by the end of the week unless the other deadlines can be moved back.
   b. Check with the other paralegals to find out if someone can help him.
   c. Be thankful the attorney has so much faith in him; he will work as much overtime as necessary to get the job done.
   d. Break down exactly how long it will take, then meet with the attorney and discuss priorities and re-assigning part of the other work.

*Read this passage and select the best answer to each question that follows.*
   PATRICK KENNEDY, PETITIONER *v.* LOUISIANA
   ON WRIT OF CERTIORARI TO THE SUPREME COURT OF
   LOUISIANA
   [June 25, 2008]
   JUSTICE KENNEDY delivered the opinion of the Court.
   The National Government and, beyond it, the separate
   States are bound by the proscriptive mandates of the

*Copyright © Mometrix Media. You have been licensed one copy of this document for personal use only. Any other reproduction or redistribution is strictly prohibited. All rights reserved.*

Eighth Amendment to the Constitution of the United States, and all persons within those respective jurisdictions may invoke its protection. See Amdts. 8 and 14, §1; *Robinson* v. *California*, 370 U. S. 660 (1962). Patrick Kennedy, the petitioner here, seeks to set aside his death sentence under the Eighth Amendment. He was charged by the respondent, the State of Louisiana, with the aggravated rape of his then-8-year-old stepdaughter. After a jury trial petitioner was convicted and sentenced to death under a state statute authorizing capital punishment for the rape of a child under 12 years of age. See La. Stat. Ann. §14:42 (West 1997 and Supp. 1998). This case presents the question whether the Constitution bars respondent from imposing the death penalty for the rape of a child where the crime did not result, and was not intended to result, in death of the victim. We hold the Eighth Amendment prohibits the death penalty for this offense. The Louisiana statute is unconstitutional.

18. The major point of Justice Kennedy's opinion in *Kennedy v. Louisiana* is that...
    a. *Robinson v. California* set a judicial precedent for the case.
    b. The Eighth Amendment prohibits cruel and unusual punishment.
    c. Patrick Kennedy seeks to set aside his death penalty.
    d. The death penalty should not be imposed for a crime that did not result in the death of the victim.

19. True or false. A Louisiana statute warrants the death penalty for child rape.

20. True or false. All states must enforce the provisions of the Eighth Amendment.

21. The Statutes at Large
    a. Contains state statutes.
    b. Is compiled chronologically.
    c. Is the official reporter for the U.S. Supreme Court.
    d. None of the above

22. West's American Digest System...
    a. Contains brief summaries of the points of law in a given case.
    b. Uses a topic and key number system
    c. Contains a descriptive word index.
    d. All of the above

23. True or false. A praecipe is a writ ordering a person to appear in court.

24. True or false. A principal stated in the opinion of a judge is called jurisprudence.

Copyright © Mometrix Media. You have been licensed one copy of this document for personal use only. Any other reproduction or redistribution is strictly prohibited. All rights reserved.

*Edit the following citation to show the correct citation form. If the citation is correct as written, write the word* correct *before the question number.*

25. *Switz v. Padre,* 217 N.E. 706 (2010)

26. A United States citizen cannot be denied the right to vote on account of gender by reason of the provision of which amendment to the U.S. Constitution?
    a. The Fourth Amendment
    b. The Fifth Amendment
    c. The Fourteenth Amendment
    d. The Nineteenth Amendment

27. In order for the Supreme Court to hear an appeal, one must...
    a. File a petition for a writ of certiorari.
    b. File a petition of mandamus.
    c. File a case of first impression.
    d. None of the above

28. True or false. Subject matter jurisdiction is a requirement that the court has the power to hear the claim that is brought before it.

29. True or false. Adjudication is a sworn statement, made in writing.

30. True or false. Article 3 of the U.S. Constitution delineates the authority of the Executive Branch of the government.

31. Which of the following is the federal law that regulates how government agencies can establish rules?
    a. Code of Federal Regulations
    b. Agricultural Act of 1949
    c. Administrative Procedure Act
    d. None of the above

32. True or false. *Marbury v. Madison* was an affirmation of the concept of judicial review.

33. True or false. Debts brought on by fraud are dischargeable.

Copyright © Mometrix Media. You have been licensed one copy of this document for personal use only. Any other reproduction or redistribution is strictly prohibited. All rights reserved.

34. A bankruptcy estate includes all of a debtor's property, with the exception of which of the following?
   a. Power of appointment in a will
   b. Interest in a non-residential lease
   c. Property acquired within 180 days after the order of relief
   d. All of the above
   e. Two of the above

35. In a Chapter 13 bankruptcy, the trustee's role is to...
   a. Distribute proceeds from sale of property.
   b. Examine and contest creditor claims.
   c. Ensure compliance of all applicable laws and procedures.
   d. Refer the client to a credit counseling agency.
   e. None of the above

36. True or false. Due to the business judgment rule, a shareholder has no recourse if a corporate officer or director acts imprudently.

37. True or false. A Chapter S corporation cannot have more than 100 shareholders.

38. The Federal Rules of Civil Procedure (FRCP) are...
   a. Applicable to lawsuits in U.S. district courts.
   b. Meant to secure the speedy determination of every proceeding.
   c. A replacement for common-law pleading.
   d. None of the above
   e. All of the above

39. True or false. A motion for new trial in a federal court must be filed within 30 days after judgment has been entered.

40. An ex delicto is...
   a. In the act of committing a crime.
   b. A matter arising from a tort.
   c. In equal guilt.
   d. After the fact.
   e. None of the above

41. True or false. Under the provisions of the Uniform Commercial Code (U.C.C.), an anticipatory repudiation means assets are not delivered in a bulk sale.

42. True or false. An individual who wants to transfer his rights under a valid contract should draw up a quitclaim deed.

43. True or false. A federal grand jury does not determine guilt or innocence.

Copyright © Mometrix Media. You have been licensed one copy of this document for personal use only. Any other reproduction or redistribution is strictly prohibited. All rights reserved.

44. A writ of habeas corpus is...
    a. Used to investigate if a person's detainment is lawful.
    b. A civil action against a state agent.
    c. Based on English common law.
    d. All of the above
    e. None of the above

45. A self-proving will is best defined as...
    a. A will that shortens the time an estate is in probate.
    b. A will that was witnessed by a person who certifies it was signed by the testator.
    c. A will that is nuncupative.
    d. All of the above
    e. Two of the above

46. True or false. The escheatment process includes drawing up a codicil.

47. True or false. The doctrine of res ipso loquitor provides the foundation for no-fault divorce.

48. True or false. Children of an annulment ordered by the court are considered to be illegitimate.

49. True or false. A balloon mortgage is a non-amortizing loan.

50. Scienter can be defined as...
    a. Guilty knowledge.
    b. Separation.
    c. Restitution.
    d. Two of the above
    e. None of the above

Copyright © Mometrix Media. You have been licensed one copy of this document for personal use only. Any other reproduction or redistribution is strictly prohibited. All rights reserved.

## Answers and Explanations

1. A: The sentence is clearly verbose. It would suffice to simply say "We must examine all the facts first."

2. A: Use of the adjective "neither" together with the conjunction "nor" does not make the subject plural. The subject is singular, so the correct verb would be "was."

3. Lying: The verb "lying" means to be in a reclining position, while "laying" means placing a person or an object somewhere.

4. D: "Respondeat superior" is Latin for "Let the master answer," and is a common legal term; legal terms do not need to be capitalized. In choice A, the phrase "not discussed in class" is correctly set off by commas. "Liable" is correctly used as an adjective in choice B. In choice C, the pronoun "who" is the correct choice because it is used as a subject. And because there is an error, choice E is not applicable.

5. False: It is not the duty of a paralegal to make assumptions. In this example, taking down a witness's statement accurately is what an attorney would expect, and nothing more.

6. C: UPL statutes are intended to discourage paralegals from any unauthorized practice of law. The UPL is clearly not meant for a paralegal to practice law and accept cases. Complying with a client's request for information is applicable to an attorney, not a paralegal. Because choice C is correct, choices D and E are incorrect.

7. False: Giving legal advice to clients directly, regardless of whether the advice is free, is a violation of the UPL and subjects the paralegal to criminal prosecution and/or termination of employment, as well as possible civil liability to the client.

8. D: Both reviewing a client's complaint and explaining to a client what appeal procedures exist for a client are completely ethical. Choice B, helping a client execute a will, is unethical. Because two answer choices are right, choice E is incorrect.

9. E: A Chinese Wall is defined by all of the statements: it prohibits the flow of information, prevents a potential conflict of interest, and isolates a lawyer or paralegal who has come from another firm that had a differing viewpoint on a case.

10. C: According to the American Bar Association Model Rules of Professional Conduct, client funds should be kept separate from operating account funds. Treasury Department Circular No. 230 explains the regulations for attorneys who appear before the IRS. The IRS has no rules concerning client funds. Because only choice C is correct, choices D and E are both incorrect.

Copyright © Mometrix Media. You have been licensed one copy of this document for personal use only. Any other reproduction or redistribution is strictly prohibited. All rights reserved.

11. True: It is allowable for a paralegal to exercise independent thinking in procedural matters; in fact, the supervising attorney should encourage it, as long as all issues are ultimately approved by the attorney.

12. False: Turning in co-workers is not the way to build a good relationship with those around you. It would be a display of poor judgment. Rumors are not facts; the best course of action would be to let the matter pass.

13. C: In a police station, a precinct is the domain of a captain; it is where he works. The same is true of the relationship between a hospital and a surgeon, in that a hospital is the domain of a surgeon. In choice A, a policeman has a beat, so the analogy is reversed and thus incorrect. A president is above congress, so choice B is not correct. And in choice D, a manager and a director are basically the same thing.

14. D: By asking Joel how she can help, Veronica has identified a problem without offending him or undermining his authority. If a senior partner were to get involved, as in choice A, the situation would not be remedied; Joel would most likely feel vindictive towards Veronica, and the situation would not improve. Choices B and C both leave the issue unresolved and thus would not help Veronica develop professionally.

15. B: Mathematically, 9 = 6 x 1.5, and 21 = 14 x 1.5. In choice A, 12 is divided by 1.5. Choice C has a multiplier of 3, and choice D simply adds 8.

16. C: The logical conclusion, after analyzing the propositions, is that some shih tzus are good at agility. There is no proposition that says no grey dogs are good at agility, or that a grey dog is not good at agility. It doesn't make sense to say that all grey dogs are shih tzus, and all shih tzus can't logically be good at agility.

17. D: Identifying the main and secondary issues is the best route to follow, and indicates the paralegal is learning how to responsibly manage his time. Choice A might result in the attorney having a lower esteem for Leonid. Finding someone else to do the work, as in choice B, would also not be a wise decision. By choosing choice C, Leonid would likely make errors that could be costly.

18. D: It clearly states in the last two sentences of the opinion that the death penalty is prohibited for the crime involved. *Robinson v. California* was not a precedent; it is only cited, along with the Eighth and Fourteenth Amendments. Choice B is not correct; the Eighth Amendment prohibits cruel and unusual punishment. And the case of *Kennedy v. Louisiana* before the Supreme Court is the appeal of Patrick Kennedy to set aside his death penalty.

19. True: The plaintiff was convicted and sentenced to death for the rape of a child under the age of 12.

Copyright © Mometrix Media. You have been licensed one copy of this document for personal use only. Any other reproduction or redistribution is strictly prohibited. All rights reserved.

20. True: The opinion begins with the statement that both the National Government and the States are bound by the mandate of the Eighth Amendment.

21. B: The Statutes at Large, which contains Federal session laws, is compiled chronologically. State statutes are listed by jurisdiction. The official reporter for the U.S. Supreme Court is *United States Reports.* Choice D is incorrect because there was a correct answer.

22. D: The American Digest System, an index of all the case law in the U.S., contains brief summaries of cases. It features a descriptive index to make a researcher's job easier, and it utilizes a topic and key number system.

23. True: "Praecipe," which is Latin for "to give an order," is one type of legal procedure whereby the court orders someone to appear in court. It can also be an order by the court clerk to issue a summons.

24. False: An opinion of a judge is a precedent. Stemming from the Latin "juris prudentia," which means "study of law," "jurisprudence" is the philosophy of law.

25. The citation is correct as written. No change is needed.

26. D: The 19th Amendment, which was ratified in 1920 (42 years after first being introduced in Congress), gave women the right to vote. The Fourth Amendment specifies that no person can be subjected to unreasonable search. The Fifth Amendment states that no person is required to testify against himself. The Fourteenth Amendment says that no person can be denied equal protection under the law.

27. A: A writ of certiorari must be filed. "Certiorari" is Latin for "to inform," and a writ of certiorari is a petition informing the Court of a request for a review. Mandamus is a writ that compels an official to perform an act. A case of first impression is when an interpretation of the law is presented in a way that has never been used before. Because there is one correct answer, choice D cannot be correct.

28. True: Subject matter jurisdiction, as compared to personal jurisdiction, means a court must have the power to hear a claim. The parties involved cannot wave subject matter jurisdiction, while personal jurisdiction can be waived. The court can dismiss the case sua sponte ("on its own") if it lacks subject matter jurisdiction.

29. False: Adjudication is a hearing and ruling on a case using judicial procedures. An affidavit is a sworn statement made in writing, usually before a notary public.

30. False: Article 3 is concerned with the Judicial Branch of government, including judicial powers, jurisdiction, and treason. The Executive Branch is treated in Article 2, the Legislative Branch in Article 1.

*Copyright © Mometrix Media. You have been licensed one copy of this document for personal use only. Any other reproduction or redistribution is strictly prohibited. All rights reserved.*

31. C: is the correct choice. The Administrative Procedure Act, passed by Congress in 1946, is the law that sets how government agencies can propose and establish regulations. The code of Federal Regulations is the codification of administrative law, published in the *Federal Register.* The Agricultural Act of 1949 stipulates that surplus food can be donated to friendly countries. Because there is a correct answer, choice D is incorrect.

32. True: In a case before the Supreme Court in 1803, *Marbury v. Madison,* Chief Justice John Marshall overturned legislation enacted in 1789, ruling that it was unconstitutional, greatly strengthening the power of the judicial branch of the government.

33. False: Debt incurred by fraud, embezzlement or larceny are non-dischargeable under the Bankruptcy Code, and the creditor has to file an adversary proceeding in the case.

34. E: The bankruptcy estate excludes a power held by a debtor for the benefit of a third party, such as the power of appointment in a will and any interest in a non-residential lease, as long as the lease expired before debtor's filing. The estate does include property acquired with 180 days after the order of relief.

35. B: In a Chapter 13 bankruptcy, the trustee is appointed to make sure that all of the creditors have valid claims. Choice A applies to a Chapter 7, when property is sold. The Department of Justice ensures compliance through its U.S. Trustee Program. It is unlikely that a trustee would refer a person already in bankruptcy to a credit counseling agency.

36. False: The court has concluded in recent cases that the business judgment rule does not always offer protection when an officer or a director fails to act prudently in making management decisions.

37. True: According to U.S. Code, a Chapter S corporation must not have more than 100 shareholders to qualify for the tax benefits allowed by the IRS.

38. E: The Federal Rules of Civil Procedure (FRCP), first established in 1938, govern civil lawsuits in U.S. district courts. According to Rule 1 of Title 1 of the FRCP, "They should be construed and administered to secure the just, speedy, and inexpensive determination of every action and proceeding." The FRCP replaced the concept of common-law pleading.

39. False: Rule 59 states that a motion for a new trial must be filed within 10 days of entry of judgment.

*Copyright © Mometrix Media. You have been licensed one copy of this document for personal use only. Any other reproduction or redistribution is strictly prohibited. All rights reserved.*

40. B: "Ex delicto" is Latin for "from a wrong." It is a legal term for a matter arising from a tort. The term for "in the act of committing a crime" is flagrante delicto. Pari delicto is "in equal guilt." "After the fact" is post factum. Because there is a correct choice, choice E is not correct.

41. False: An anticipatory repudiation is a denial by a party to a contract to perform his or her contractual obligations; it is defined in Article 2A, Leases, of the U.C.C., and does not apply to bulk sales.

42. False: Someone who wants to transfer his rights in a contract should draft an assignment, where the assignor transfers rights to the assignee. A quitclaim deed is a real property deed that offers no warranty on whether the title is valid or not.

43. True: A grand jury determines if probable cause exists that a crime was indeed perpetrated by the person being investigated; if it does, it returns an indictment or a written charge to that effect.

44. D: Habeas corpus (Latin for "you have the body") is used to bring a prisoner or other detainee (such as a mental patient) before the court to determine the legality of the detainment. As such, it is a civil action against a state agent (i.e., a warden). The concept of habeas corpus originated in English common law.

45. A: A self-proving will shortens the length of time an estate is in probate because it is easy for the court to determine it is indeed the true last will and testament of the deceased. A self-proving will must be witnessed by at least two people who certify it was signed by the decedent. A nuncupative will is an oral statement made on a death bed before witnesses. Because there is only one correct choice, choices D and E are both incorrect.

46. False: Escheatment is the ability of the state to obtain title to property of an individual who dies intestate, or without a will or any heirs. A codicil is a supplement to a will, so the two are contradictory.

47. False: The doctrine of res ipso loquitor (Latin for "the thing speaks for itself") holds that an individual is responsible for an injury if the most probable cause was that person's negligence. It has nothing to do with no-fault divorce.

48. False: An annulment that dissolves a marriage does not recognize any children of that marriage to be illegitimate. Also, just like in a divorce, custody, child support and alimony can be determined by the court.

49. True: A balloon mortgage is a loan that is non-amortizing. At the end of the term there is still a principal amount left which must be paid off or refinanced. Balloon mortgages are usually short term, five years or less, for instance.

Copyright © Mometrix Media. You have been licensed one copy of this document for personal use only. Any other reproduction or redistribution is strictly prohibited. All rights reserved.

50. A: "Scienter," which means "knowingly" in Latin, is guilty knowledge, and is enough to charge someone with a crime. In a 1976 ruling, the U.S. Supreme Court described scienter as "a mental state embracing intent to deceive, manipulate, or defraud." Separation is a state of being apart; it can also refer to legal separation of a married couple. "Restitution" does not correctly describe "scienter"; it means restoration of property or compensation for loss. Because there is only one correct answer, choices D and E are both incorrect.

Copyright © Mometrix Media. You have been licensed one copy of this document for personal use only. Any other reproduction or redistribution is strictly prohibited. All rights reserved.

# Secret Key #1 - Time is Your Greatest Enemy

## *Pace Yourself*

Wear a watch. At the beginning of the test, check the time (or start a chronometer on your watch to count the minutes), and check the time after every few questions to make sure you are "on schedule."

If you are forced to speed up, do it efficiently. Usually one or more answer choices can be eliminated without too much difficulty. Above all, don't panic. Don't speed up and just begin guessing at random choices. By pacing yourself, and continually monitoring your progress against your watch, you will always know exactly how far ahead or behind you are with your available time. If you find that you are one minute behind on the test, don't skip one question without spending any time on it, just to catch back up. Take 15 fewer seconds on the next four questions, and after four questions you'll have caught back up. Once you catch back up, you can continue working each problem at your normal pace.

Furthermore, don't dwell on the problems that you were rushed on. If a problem was taking up too much time and you made a hurried guess, it must be difficult. The difficult questions are the ones you are most likely to miss anyway, so it isn't a big loss. It is better to end with more time than you need than to run out of time.

Lastly, sometimes it is beneficial to slow down if you are constantly getting ahead of time. You are always more likely to catch a careless mistake by working more slowly than quickly, and among very high-scoring test takers (those who are likely to have lots of time left over), careless errors affect the score more than mastery of material.

*Copyright © Mometrix Media. You have been licensed one copy of this document for personal use only. Any other reproduction or redistribution is strictly prohibited. All rights reserved.*

# Secret Key #2 - Guessing is not Guesswork

You probably know that guessing is a good idea - unlike other standardized tests, there is no penalty for getting a wrong answer. Even if you have no idea about a question, you still have a 20-25% chance of getting it right.

Most test takers do not understand the impact that proper guessing can have on their score. Unless you score extremely high, guessing will significantly contribute to your final score.

## Monkeys Take the Test

What most test takers don't realize is that to insure that 20-25% chance, you have to guess randomly. If you put 20 monkeys in a room to take this test, assuming they answered once per question and behaved themselves, on average they would get 20-25% of the questions correct. Put 20 test takers in the room, and the average will be much lower among guessed questions. Why?

1. The test writers intentionally writes deceptive answer choices that "look" right. A test taker has no idea about a question, so picks the "best looking" answer, which is often wrong. The monkey has no idea what looks good and what doesn't, so will consistently be lucky about 20-25% of the time.
2. Test takers will eliminate answer choices from the guessing pool based on a hunch or intuition. Simple but correct answers often get excluded, leaving a 0% chance of being correct. The monkey has no clue, and often gets lucky with the best choice.

This is why the process of elimination endorsed by most test courses is flawed and detrimental to your performance- test takers don't guess, they make an ignorant stab in the dark that is usually worse than random.

Copyright © Mometrix Media. You have been licensed one copy of this document for personal use only. Any other reproduction or redistribution is strictly prohibited. All rights reserved.

# $5 Challenge

Let me introduce one of the most valuable ideas of this course- the $5 challenge:

*You only mark your "best guess" if you are willing to bet $5 on it.*
*You only eliminate choices from guessing if you are willing to bet $5 on it.*

Why $5? Five dollars is an amount of money that is small yet not insignificant, and can really add up fast (20 questions could cost you $100). Likewise, each answer choice on one question of the test will have a small impact on your overall score, but it can really add up to a lot of points in the end.

The process of elimination IS valuable. The following shows your chance of guessing it right:

| If you eliminate wrong answer choices until only this many answer choices remain: | 1 | 2 | 3 |
|---|---|---|---|
| Chance of getting it correct: | 100% | 50% | 33% |

However, if you accidentally eliminate the right answer or go on a hunch for an incorrect answer, your chances drop dramatically: to 0%. By guessing among all the answer choices, you are GUARANTEED to have a shot at the right answer.

That's why the $5 test is so valuable- if you give up the advantage and safety of a pure guess, it had better be worth the risk.

What we still haven't covered is how to be sure that whatever guess you make is truly random. Here's the easiest way:

*Always pick the first answer choice among those remaining.*

Such a technique means that you have decided, **before you see a single test question**, exactly how you are going to guess- and since the order of choices tells you nothing about which one is correct, this guessing technique is perfectly random.

This section is not meant to scare you away from making educated guesses or eliminating choices- you just need to define when a choice is worth eliminating. The $5 test, along with a pre-defined random guessing strategy, is the best way to make sure you reap all of the benefits of guessing.

Copyright © Mometrix Media. You have been licensed one copy of this document for personal use only. Any other reproduction or redistribution is strictly prohibited. All rights reserved.

# Secret Key #3 - Practice Smarter, Not Harder

Many test takers delay the test preparation process because they dread the awful amounts of practice time they think necessary to succeed on the test. We have refined an effective method that will take you only a fraction of the time.

There are a number of "obstacles" in your way to succeed. Among these are answering questions, finishing in time, and mastering test-taking strategies. All must be executed on the day of the test at peak performance, or your score will suffer. The test is a mental marathon that has a large impact on your future.

Just like a marathon runner, it is important to work your way up to the full challenge. So first you just worry about questions, and then time, and finally strategy:

## *Success Strategy*

1. Find a good source for practice tests.
2. If you are willing to make a larger time investment, consider using more than one study guide- often the different approaches of multiple authors will help you "get" difficult concepts.
3. Take a practice test with no time constraints, with all study helps "open book." Take your time with questions and focus on applying strategies.
4. Take a practice test with time constraints, with all guides "open book."
5. Take a final practice test with no open material and time limits

If you have time to take more practice tests, just repeat step 5. By gradually exposing yourself to the full rigors of the test environment, you will condition your mind to the stress of test day and maximize your success.

*Copyright © Mometrix Media. You have been licensed one copy of this document for personal use only. Any other reproduction or redistribution is strictly prohibited. All rights reserved.*

# Secret Key #4 - Prepare, Don't Procrastinate

Let me state an obvious fact: if you take the test three times, you will get three different scores. This is due to the way you feel on test day, the level of preparedness you have, and, despite the test writers' claims to the contrary, some tests WILL be easier for you than others.

Since your future depends so much on your score, you should maximize your chances of success. In order to maximize the likelihood of success, you've got to prepare in advance. This means taking practice tests and spending time learning the information and test taking strategies you will need to succeed.

Never take the test as a "practice" test, expecting that you can just take it again if you need to. Feel free to take sample tests on your own, but when you go to take the official test, be prepared, be focused, and do your best the first time!

Copyright © Mometrix Media. You have been licensed one copy of this document for personal use only. Any other reproduction or redistribution is strictly prohibited. All rights reserved.

# Secret Key #5 - Test Yourself

Everyone knows that time is money. There is no need to spend too much of your time or too little of your time preparing for the test. You should only spend as much of your precious time preparing as is necessary for you to get the score you need.

Once you have taken a practice test under real conditions of time constraints, then you will know if you are ready for the test or not.

If you have scored extremely high the first time that you take the practice test, then there is not much point in spending countless hours studying. You are already there.

Benchmark your abilities by retaking practice tests and seeing how much you have improved. Once you score high enough to guarantee success, then you are ready.

If you have scored well below where you need, then knuckle down and begin studying in earnest. Check your improvement regularly through the use of practice tests under real conditions. Above all, don't worry, panic, or give up. The key is perseverance!

Then, when you go to take the test, remain confident and remember how well you did on the practice tests. If you can score high enough on a practice test, then you can do the same on the real thing.

*Copyright © Mometrix Media. You have been licensed one copy of this document for personal use only. Any other reproduction or redistribution is strictly prohibited. All rights reserved.*

# General Strategies

The most important thing you can do is to ignore your fears and jump into the test immediately- do not be overwhelmed by any strange-sounding terms. You have to jump into the test like jumping into a pool- all at once is the easiest way.

## Make Predictions

As you read and understand the question, try to guess what the answer will be. Remember that several of the answer choices are wrong, and once you begin reading them, your mind will immediately become cluttered with answer choices designed to throw you off. Your mind is typically the most focused immediately after you have read the question and digested its contents. If you can, try to predict what the correct answer will be. You may be surprised at what you can predict.

Quickly scan the choices and see if your prediction is in the listed answer choices. If it is, then you can be quite confident that you have the right answer. It still won't hurt to check the other answer choices, but most of the time, you've got it!

## Answer the Question

It may seem obvious to only pick answer choices that answer the question, but the test writers can create some excellent answer choices that are wrong. Don't pick an answer just because it sounds right, or you believe it to be true. It MUST answer the question. Once you've made your selection, always go back and check it against the question and make sure that you didn't misread the question, and the answer choice does answer the question posed.

## Benchmark

After you read the first answer choice, decide if you think it sounds correct or not. If it doesn't, move on to the next answer choice. If it does, mentally mark that answer choice. This doesn't mean that you've definitely selected it as your answer choice, it just means that it's the best you've seen thus far. Go ahead and read the next choice. If the next choice is worse than the one you've already selected, keep going to the next answer choice. If the next choice is better than the choice you've already selected, mentally mark the new answer choice as your best guess.

The first answer choice that you select becomes your standard. Every other answer choice must be benchmarked against that standard. That choice is correct until proven otherwise by another answer choice beating it out. Once you've decided that no other answer choice seems as good, do one final check to ensure that your answer choice answers the question posed.

*Copyright © Mometrix Media. You have been licensed one copy of this document for personal use only. Any other reproduction or redistribution is strictly prohibited. All rights reserved.*

## Valid Information

Don't discount any of the information provided in the question. Every piece of information may be necessary to determine the correct answer. None of the information in the question is there to throw you off (while the answer choices will certainly have information to throw you off). If two seemingly unrelated topics are discussed, don't ignore either. You can be confident there is a relationship, or it wouldn't be included in the question, and you are probably going to have to determine what is that relationship to find the answer.

## Avoid "Fact Traps"

Don't get distracted by a choice that is factually true. Your search is for the answer that answers the question. Stay focused and don't fall for an answer that is true but incorrect. Always go back to the question and make sure you're choosing an answer that actually answers the question and is not just a true statement. An answer can be factually correct, but it MUST answer the question asked. Additionally, two answers can both be seemingly correct, so be sure to read all of the answer choices, and make sure that you get the one that BEST answers the question.

## Milk the Question

Some of the questions may throw you completely off. They might deal with a subject you have not been exposed to, or one that you haven't reviewed in years. While your lack of knowledge about the subject will be a hindrance, the question itself can give you many clues that will help you find the correct answer. Read the question carefully and look for clues. Watch particularly for adjectives and nouns describing difficult terms or words that you don't recognize. Regardless of if you completely understand a word or not, replacing it with a synonym either provided or one you more familiar with may help you to understand what the questions are asking. Rather than wracking your mind about specific detailed information concerning a difficult term or word, try to use mental substitutes that are easier to understand.

## The Trap of Familiarity

Don't just choose a word because you recognize it. On difficult questions, you may not recognize a number of words in the answer choices. The test writers don't put "make-believe" words on the test; so don't think that just because you only recognize all the words in one answer choice means that answer choice must be correct. If you only recognize words in one answer choice, then focus on that one. Is it correct? Try your best to determine if it is correct. If it is, that is great, but if it doesn't, eliminate it. Each word and answer choice you eliminate increases your chances of getting the question correct, even if you then have to guess among the unfamiliar choices.

*Copyright © Mometrix Media. You have been licensed one copy of this document for personal use only. Any other reproduction or redistribution is strictly prohibited. All rights reserved.*

## Eliminate Answers

Eliminate choices as soon as you realize they are wrong. But be careful! Make sure you consider all of the possible answer choices. Just because one appears right, doesn't mean that the next one won't be even better! The test writers will usually put more than one good answer choice for every question, so read all of them. Don't worry if you are stuck between two that seem right. By getting down to just two remaining possible choices, your odds are now 50/50. Rather than wasting too much time, play the odds. You are guessing, but guessing wisely, because you've been able to knock out some of the answer choices that you know are wrong. If you are eliminating choices and realize that the last answer choice you are left with is also obviously wrong, don't panic. Start over and consider each choice again. There may easily be something that you missed the first time and will realize on the second pass.

## Tough Questions

If you are stumped on a problem or it appears too hard or too difficult, don't waste time. Move on! Remember though, if you can quickly check for obviously incorrect answer choices, your chances of guessing correctly are greatly improved. Before you completely give up, at least try to knock out a couple of possible answers. Eliminate what you can and then guess at the remaining answer choices before moving on.

## Brainstorm

If you get stuck on a difficult question, spend a few seconds quickly brainstorming. Run through the complete list of possible answer choices. Look at each choice and ask yourself, "Could this answer the question satisfactorily?" Go through each answer choice and consider it independently of the other. By systematically going through all possibilities, you may find something that you would otherwise overlook. Remember that when you get stuck, it's important to try to keep moving.

## Read Carefully

Understand the problem. Read the question and answer choices carefully. Don't miss the question because you misread the terms. You have plenty of time to read each question thoroughly and make sure you understand what is being asked. Yet a happy medium must be attained, so don't waste too much time. You must read carefully, but efficiently.

## Face Value

When in doubt, use common sense. Always accept the situation in the problem at face value. Don't read too much into it. These problems will not require you to make huge leaps of logic. The test writers aren't trying to throw you off with a

Copyright © Mometrix Media. You have been licensed one copy of this document for personal use only. Any other reproduction or redistribution is strictly prohibited. All rights reserved.

cheap trick.  If you have to go beyond creativity and make a leap of logic in order to have an answer choice answer the question, then you should look at the other answer choices.  Don't overcomplicate the problem by creating theoretical relationships or explanations that will warp time or space.  These are normal problems rooted in reality.  It's just that the applicable relationship or explanation may not be readily apparent and you have to figure things out. Use your common sense to interpret anything that isn't clear.

## Prefixes

If you're having trouble with a word in the question or answer choices, try dissecting it.  Take advantage of every clue that the word might include.  Prefixes and suffixes can be a huge help.  Usually they allow you to determine a basic meaning.  Pre- means before, post- means after, pro - is positive, de- is negative.  From these prefixes and suffixes, you can get an idea of the general meaning of the word and try to put it into context.  Beware though of any traps.  Just because con is the opposite of pro, doesn't necessarily mean congress is the opposite of progress!

## Hedge Phrases

Watch out for critical "hedge" phrases, such as likely, may, can, will often, sometimes, often, almost, mostly, usually, generally, rarely, sometimes.  Question writers insert these hedge phrases to cover every possibility.  Often an answer choice will be wrong simply because it leaves no room for exception.  Avoid answer choices that have definitive words like "exactly," and "always".

## Switchback Words

Stay alert for "switchbacks".  These are the words and phrases frequently used to alert you to shifts in thought.  The most common switchback word is "but".  Others include although, however, nevertheless, on the other hand, even though, while, in spite of, despite, regardless of.

## New Information

Correct answer choices will rarely have completely new information included.  Answer choices typically are straightforward reflections of the material asked about and will directly relate to the question.  If a new piece of information is included in an answer choice that doesn't even seem to relate to the topic being asked about, then that answer choice is likely incorrect.   All of the information needed to answer the question is usually provided for you, and so you should not have to make guesses that are unsupported or choose answer choices that require unknown information that cannot be reasoned on its own.

*Copyright © Mometrix Media. You have been licensed one copy of this document for personal use only.*
*Any other reproduction or redistribution is strictly prohibited. All rights reserved.*

## Time Management

On technical questions, don't get lost on the technical terms. Don't spend too much time on any one question. If you don't know what a term means, then since you don't have a dictionary, odds are you aren't going to get much further. You should immediately recognize terms as whether or not you know them. If you don't, work with the other clues that you have, the other answer choices and terms provided, but don't waste too much time trying to figure out a difficult term.

## Contextual Clues

Look for contextual clues. An answer can be right but not correct. The contextual clues will help you find the answer that is most right and is correct. Understand the context in which a phrase or statement is made. This will help you make important distinctions.

## Don't Panic

Panicking will not answer any questions for you. Therefore, it isn't helpful. When you first see the question, if your mind goes blank, take a deep breath. Force yourself to mechanically go through the steps of solving the problem and using the strategies you've learned.

## Pace Yourself

Don't get clock fever. It's easy to be overwhelmed when you're looking at a page full of questions, your mind is full of random thoughts and feeling confused, and the clock is ticking down faster than you would like. Calm down and maintain the pace that you have set for yourself. As long as you are on track by monitoring your pace, you are guaranteed to have enough time for yourself. When you get to the last few minutes of the test, it may seem like you won't have enough time left, but if you only have as many questions as you should have left at that point, then you're right on track!

## Answer Selection

The best way to pick an answer choice is to eliminate all of those that are wrong, until only one is left and confirm that is the correct answer. Sometimes though, an answer choice may immediately look right. Be careful! Take a second to make sure that the other choices are not equally obvious. Don't make a hasty mistake. There are only two times that you should stop before checking other answers. First is when you are positive that the answer choice you have selected is correct. Second is when time is almost out and you have to make a quick guess!

Copyright © Mometrix Media. You have been licensed one copy of this document for personal use only. Any other reproduction or redistribution is strictly prohibited. All rights reserved.

## Check Your Work

Since you will probably not know every term listed and the answer to every question, it is important that you get credit for the ones that you do know. Don't miss any questions through careless mistakes. If at all possible, try to take a second to look back over your answer selection and make sure you've selected the correct answer choice and haven't made a costly careless mistake (such as marking an answer choice that you didn't mean to mark). This quick double check should more than pay for itself in caught mistakes for the time it costs.

## Beware of Directly Quoted Answers

Sometimes an answer choice will repeat word for word a portion of the question or reference section. However, beware of such exact duplication – it may be a trap! More than likely, the correct choice will paraphrase or summarize a point, rather than being exactly the same wording.

## Slang

Scientific sounding answers are better than slang ones. An answer choice that begins "To compare the outcomes…" is much more likely to be correct than one that begins "Because some people insisted…"

## Extreme Statements

Avoid wild answers that throw out highly controversial ideas that are proclaimed as established fact. An answer choice that states the "process should be used in certain situations, if…" is much more likely to be correct than one that states the "process should be discontinued completely." The first is a calm rational statement and doesn't even make a definitive, uncompromising stance, using a hedge word "if" to provide wiggle room, whereas the second choice is a radical idea and far more extreme.

## Answer Choice Families

When you have two or more answer choices that are direct opposites or parallels, one of them is usually the correct answer. For instance, if one answer choice states "x increases" and another answer choice states "x decreases" or "y increases," then those two or three answer choices are very similar in construction and fall into the same family of answer choices. A family of answer choices is when two or three answer choices are very similar in construction, and yet often have a directly opposite meaning. Usually the correct answer choice will be in that family of answer choices. The "odd man out" or answer choice that doesn't seem to fit the parallel construction of the other answer choices is more likely to be incorrect.

*Copyright © Mometrix Media. You have been licensed one copy of this document for personal use only. Any other reproduction or redistribution is strictly prohibited. All rights reserved.*

# Special Report: Additional Bonus Material

Due to our efforts to try to keep this book to a manageable length, we've created a link that will give you access to all of your additional bonus material.

Please visit http://www.mometrix.com/bonus948/clacp to access the information.

Copyright © Mometrix Media. You have been licensed one copy of this document for personal use only. Any other reproduction or redistribution is strictly prohibited. All rights reserved.